I0409270

CONSULTING
UNCOMPLICATED

A Comprehensive Guide to Launching and Scaling Your Consulting Business

Copyright © 2023 by **Richmond Lee**

All rights reserved.

Contents

INTRODUCTION

Welcome to the world of limitless possibilities—the realm of consulting entrepreneurship. This journey you're embarking on is not just about building a business; it's about crafting a legacy of impact and innovation. In these pages, we'll unravel the secrets to simplifying the intricate art of consulting, guiding you from the very first spark of an idea to the exhilarating heights of a thriving consultancy.

Picture a world where uncertainty becomes a playground for creativity, where challenges are transformed into stepping stones, and where your expertise finds its true purpose. Within these chapters, we'll explore the power of the entrepreneurial mindset, help you define your unique niche, and reveal strategies to conquer the daunting financial risks that come with the territory.

Discover how to captivate your audience with compelling stories, redefine the way you deliver value, and forge unbreakable client relationships that stand the test of time. As you walk this path, you'll also learn the art of scaling gracefully, navigating the delicate balance between professional excellence and personal well-being.

But this journey isn't just about success; it's about embracing the lessons failure brings, forming alliances with mentors and like-minded peers, and leaving an indelible mark on the world. The pages ahead are a tapestry woven with insights from seasoned consultants, hard-won wisdom from the entrepreneurial front lines, and a roadmap that will lead you to transcend boundaries you never thought possible.

So, whether you're at the cusp of diving into the consultancy world or seeking to invigorate your existing venture, buckle up—this guide is your compass, your confidant, and your catalyst for transformation. The voyage to becoming an unstoppable force in the consulting arena begins now.

Chapter 1:

The Essence of Consulting Entrepreneurship

In the heart of every successful consulting venture lies a potent blend of expertise, vision, and a dash of audacity. This chapter is your gateway to understanding the very essence of consulting entrepreneurship—the unique alchemy that propels you from a mere idea to a thriving business.

Navigating the Consulting Landscape

Venturing into the world of consulting is akin to stepping onto a vast and uncharted landscape. We'll be your guide, helping you decipher the intricacies, understand the nuances, and illuminate the path forward. Learn how consulting differs from other business models and gain insights into why your expertise holds the power to create transformative change.

Embracing the Entrepreneurial Mindset

At the core of every successful consultant is an entrepreneurial mindset—a way of thinking that embraces uncertainty as opportunity, failure as a stepping stone, and challenges as catalysts for growth. Discover the traits that set entrepreneurs apart and unlock the mindset that will propel your consulting journey.

From uncovering your niche to grasping the pulse of the market, Chapter 1 sets the stage for the enlightening journey that awaits. As you delve into the heart of consulting entrepreneurship, remember that here, in this chapter, you're laying the cornerstone for the consultancy you're about to build—a venture brimming with potential, purpose, and unparalleled possibility.

Traits for Success: Nurturing the Entrepreneurial Spirit

In the realm of consulting entrepreneurship, success isn't solely determined by strategies and tactics; it's also shaped by the qualities that reside within the entrepreneur. As you embark on this transformative journey, cultivating these key traits will be your compass, guiding you toward achievement and fulfillment.

1. Visionary Thinking

Successful consultants possess the ability to see beyond the immediate horizon. They envision innovative solutions, anticipate industry shifts, and craft a future where their expertise plays a pivotal role. A visionary mindset fuels the passion and determination needed to overcome challenges and create lasting impact

2. Resilience and Adaptability

In the face of adversity, resilience is the shield that guards your dreams. Entrepreneurs in the consulting arena encounter setbacks and obstacles, but it's their resilience that keeps them forging ahead. The willingness to adapt, pivot, and learn from failures is what sets apart those who merely survive from those who truly thrive.

3. Customer-Centric Focus

Clients are at the heart of consulting success. Exceptional consultants listen intently, empathize deeply, and tailor their solutions to address the specific needs of their clients. A customer-centric approach not only builds trust but also paves the way for enduring relationships and a sterling reputation.

4. Continuous Learning

The consultancy landscape is dynamic and ever-evolving. Those who stay ahead are the ones committed to continuous learning. Embrace new trends, technologies, and methodologies. By remaining a perpetual student of your field, you position yourself as an authority, offering clients the most innovative and effective solutions.

5. Strategic Risk-Taking

Calculated risks are the foundation of growth. Entrepreneurs who dare to venture into uncharted territory often reap the greatest rewards. Strategic risk-taking involves weighing potential benefits against potential downsides and having the courage to take action when the odds are in your favor.

6. Networking and Relationship Building

In the interconnected world of consulting, relationships are gold. Building a robust network of mentors, collaborators, and industry peers provides a safety net of advice, support, and potential partnerships. These connections can open doors, offer guidance, and elevate your consultancy to new heights.

7. Self-Motivation

As an entrepreneur, you are your own driving force. The ability to set goals, stay focused, and maintain enthusiasm even in the face of monotony is a hallmark of successful consultants. Self-motivation keeps you on track, propelling you through both mundane tasks and groundbreaking endeavors.

8. Problem-Solving Prowess

Consulting is, at its core, about solving complex problems. Possessing a sharp analytical mind, the ability to dissect issues, and a knack for innovative problem-solving are the tools that equip you to provide invaluable solutions to your clients.

9. Integrity and Ethics

Trust is the cornerstone of any consultancy. Upholding high ethical standards and demonstrating integrity in all your dealings establishes credibility, fosters long-term relationships, and reinforces your reputation as a trustworthy consultant.

These traits, woven together, form the fabric of a successful consultant's character. As you cultivate these qualities within yourself, you're not only nurturing your personal growth but also laying a solid foundation for a consulting venture that's destined to thrive.

From Struggles to Triumph: Sarah's Journey of Resilience

Meet Sarah Thompson, a tenacious consultant who personifies the traits for success. Sarah's journey began in the heart of uncertainty, where her resilience, adaptability, and visionary thinking paved the way for her triumph.

After years of working as an environmental scientist, Sarah identified a gap in the market for sustainable business consulting. She envisioned a future where companies embraced eco-friendly practices not just for compliance, but for genuine environmental impact. With a clear vision in mind, she embarked on her entrepreneurial journey.

The road wasn't smooth. Sarah encountered setbacks and challenges that tested her resilience. Her initial pitch to potential clients was met with skepticism, but she used each rejection as an opportunity to refine her approach. She adapted her messaging, honed her solution, and learned to turn objections into chances for improvement.

Sarah's customer-centric focus was evident in every interaction. She listened intently to her clients' pain points and tailored her solutions to their unique needs. Her commitment to continuous learning meant she was always one step ahead, incorporating the latest sustainability trends and technologies into her offerings.

However, her true test came when a global economic downturn hit. Many businesses slashed their budgets, and Sarah's consulting services faced a dip in demand. Undeterred, she strategically shifted her focus to provide cost-effective solutions that helped companies navigate the crisis. Her strategic risk-taking paid off, and she emerged stronger on the other side.

Throughout her journey, Sarah's networking prowess came to the fore. She built connections with industry experts, forming partnerships that expanded her reach and enriched her knowledge. These relationships not only provided invaluable insights but also served as a support system during tough times.

Above all, Sarah's integrity shone brightly. She upheld ethical standards, offering transparent advice even when it wasn't the most profitable route. This unwavering commitment to honesty and trustworthiness solidified her reputation as a consultant who truly cared about her clients' success.

Sarah's story is a testament to the power of the traits for success. Her visionary thinking transformed an idea into a thriving consultancy. Resilience and adaptability carried her through challenges, while customer-centric focus, continuous learning, and strategic risk-taking elevated her services. Networking, self-motivation, problem-solving, and unwavering integrity rounded out her journey, painting a picture of a consultant who not only achieved success but also left an indelible mark on her field.

Sarah's journey serves as an inspiration for aspiring consultants, showcasing that with the right traits, unwavering determination, and a heart full of passion, triumph is not just a possibility—it's an inevitability.

Conclusion: Embrace Your Journey

As we conclude this chapter, the essence of consulting entrepreneurship stands illuminated. The traits that define successful entrepreneurs are not mere abstract concepts; they are the threads that weave the fabric of your journey. Visionary thinking, resilience, customer-centric focus, and the other traits we've explored are not just qualities to possess—they are the guiding stars that will lead you toward your goals.

Remember, you are embarking on a path that transcends conventional boundaries. The challenges you face will test your mettle, and the victories you achieve will be a testament to your dedication. The journey of a consultant is not a linear one; it's a tapestry of growth, learning, and evolution.

As you move forward, hold onto the knowledge that the traits for success are not static. They can be cultivated, nurtured, and expanded upon. Each challenge you overcome, each client you serve, and each new insight you gain will further refine these qualities within you.

In the chapters ahead, we will delve deeper into the intricacies of launching and growing your consulting business. We will explore the art of crafting your business foundation, conquering common challenges, forging impactful connections, and leaving a lasting legacy. The road may be winding, but armed with the traits we've discussed, you're equipped to navigate it with confidence.

So, with a heart full of purpose and the traits for success as your compass, embrace your journey as a consulting entrepreneur. The path you're treading is one of remarkable potential, and as you take each step, you're forging your own unique story of triumph, impact, and fulfillment.

Chapter 2: Defining Your Consulting Venture

In the vast landscape of consulting, finding your footing is not just about understanding the market; it's about uncovering the essence of what makes your consultancy unique. In this chapter, we delve into the crucial process of defining your consulting venture, from identifying your expertise to pinpointing your ideal client.

Identifying Your Expertise and Niche

At the heart of every successful consulting venture lies a core expertise—an area where your knowledge, skills, and passion converge. We'll guide you through the process of identifying your strengths and honing in on a specific niche within your field. Whether it's financial advisory, marketing strategy, or technological solutions, discovering your niche will give your consultancy a clear direction and a distinct voice.

Validating Market Need: Finding Your Ideal Client

Defining your consultancy isn't just about what you offer; it's about who you serve. Through market research and analysis, you'll uncover the needs, pain points, and aspirations of your target audience. We'll explore techniques to validate the demand for your services and ensure there's a receptive market for your expertise. By finding your ideal client, you'll not only sharpen your focus but also increase your chances of making a meaningful impact.

In the chapters ahead, you'll learn how to transform this foundation into a robust business model, one that resonates with your expertise and aligns with your clients' needs. The process of defining your consulting venture is not just a preliminary step; it's the cornerstone upon which your consultancy's success will be built.

Identifying Your Expertise: Uncovering Your Unique Brilliance

Discovering your expertise is like unearthing a hidden gem within yourself—one that holds the power to illuminate your consulting journey. Here's a step-by-step guide to help you identify the area where your knowledge, skills, and passion intersect, paving the way for a consultancy that's truly exceptional.

1. Reflect on Your Skills and Knowledge:

Take a moment to assess your skills, experiences, and educational background. What are you exceptionally good at? What knowledge have you accumulated over the years? Consider both your professional skills and any personal talents that could be leveraged in a consulting context.

2. Identify Your Passion:

Passion fuels purpose. Reflect on what aspects of your field or industry ignite a fire within you. What topics do you find yourself constantly researching or discussing? Your passion is a powerful indicator of where your expertise lies.

3. Analyze Your Achievements:

Review your past achievements, projects, and successes. What were the common threads that tied these accomplishments together? Were there specific areas where you consistently excelled? These patterns can reveal where your expertise naturally shines.

4. Seek Feedback:

Ask colleagues, mentors, friends, and even clients about your strengths and areas where they perceive you as an expert. Sometimes, an external perspective can provide insights you might have overlooked.

5. Assess Market Demand:

Consider the current and future demand for specific skills or knowledge within your industry. What are the pain points businesses or individuals are facing? Your expertise should align with addressing these challenges.

6. Combine Skills and Passion:

Find the sweet spot where your skills intersect with your passion. This is the zone where you'll not only excel but also find fulfillment in your consulting work.

7. Test and Refine:

Once you've identified a potential expertise area, test it out. Engage in projects, workshops, or seminars that allow you to apply and refine your skills. Feedback from these experiences will help you gauge your true expertise.

Remember, expertise is not static; it can evolve as you continue learning and growing. The goal is to identify an area where you have a unique perspective, a deep well of knowledge, and the ability to bring valuable insights to your clients. By harnessing your expertise, you're setting the stage for a consultancy that's grounded in authenticity and poised for success.

From Misaligned to Flourishing: Tom's Journey to Expertise

Tom Harrison's story is a testament to the transformative power of identifying the right expertise. Early in his career, Tom found himself in the wrong field. Armed with an engineering degree, he had ventured into a job that left him uninspired and disconnected.

For years, Tom followed a path that he believed was expected of him. But the spark was missing. He felt like a cog in a machine, going through the motions without a sense of purpose. Despite excelling in his role, he realized that expertise alone couldn't fill the void he felt.

It was during a chance conversation at a networking event that Tom's journey took an unexpected turn. Engaging with professionals from diverse fields, he discovered a common thread—he was most animated when discussing sustainability practices and environmental impact.

Tom's passion for environmental responsibility was a whisper that had been drowned out for years. As he delved deeper, he realized that his true expertise lay not in engineering alone, but at the intersection of engineering and sustainable practices. This revelation was a turning point.

He decided to pivot his career, aligning his skills with his newfound passion. Tom pursued additional education and certifications in sustainable design and green technologies. Armed with this enriched expertise, he took a leap and launched a consultancy focused on helping businesses integrate eco-friendly practices into their operations.

The shift wasn't without its challenges. Tom faced skepticism and uncertainty, but his passion and newfound expertise fueled his determination. He began by offering workshops and webinars, sharing his knowledge with businesses eager to embrace sustainability. His expertise resonated, and gradually, he started attracting clients seeking authentic guidance in navigating the world of sustainable practices.

Tom's journey from misalignment to flourishing showcased the impact of identifying the right expertise. By embracing his passion and combining it with his engineering background, he not only found fulfillment but also built a thriving consultancy that made a tangible difference.

Tom's story reminds us that expertise isn't just about what you know; it's about what makes your heart race and your spirit soar. It's about finding the sweet spot where your skills and passions converge. Tom's journey encourages us to be open to self-discovery, to listen to the whispers of our true calling, and to pursue a path that aligns with our authentic expertise.

Finding Your Ideal Client: A Blueprint for Targeted Impact

The journey of a successful consultant is not just about what you offer; it's about who you serve. Finding your ideal client involves a deliberate process of understanding your audience, empathizing with their needs, and positioning yourself to provide exceptional value. Here's a comprehensive guide to help you navigate this critical aspect of your consulting venture.

1. Define Your Client Persona:

Create a detailed profile of your ideal client. Consider demographics, industry, company size, pain points, goals, and challenges. This persona will serve as your compass, guiding your strategies and communication.

2. Conduct Market Research:

Dig deep into your industry to uncover trends, demands, and gaps. Analyze your competitors' client bases to identify underserved segments that align with your expertise.

3. Leverage Your Network:

Tap into your existing network to connect with potential clients. Attend industry events, webinars, and networking sessions to build relationships and understand the needs of your target audience.

4. Craft Tailored Solutions:

Once you've identified your ideal client, tailor your services to meet their specific needs. Your solutions should resonate with their pain points, showcasing your expertise in addressing their challenges.

5. Develop Compelling Messaging:

Craft clear and compelling messaging that speaks directly to your ideal client's pain points and aspirations. Your communication should demonstrate that you understand their unique situation and can provide the solutions they seek.

6. Utilize Online Platforms:

Leverage online platforms like social media, blogs, and industry forums to showcase your expertise and connect with potential clients. Consistent and relevant content establishes you as a trusted authority.

7. Offer Value First:

Provide value upfront through webinars, workshops, free resources, or insightful content. Demonstrating your expertise without an immediate sales pitch fosters trust and positions you as a valuable resource.

8. **Nurture Relationships:**

Building client relationships is a journey, not a transaction. Keep the lines of communication open, offer continuous support, and be genuinely invested in their success.

9. **Seek Feedback and Refine:**

Regularly seek feedback from your clients to ensure you're meeting their expectations. Use this feedback to refine your services and strengthen your client relationships.

10. **Stay Adaptable:**

Market dynamics change, and so do client needs. Stay attuned to shifts and be adaptable in fine-tuning your strategies to cater to evolving demands.

Finding your ideal client is about more than just targeting; it's about creating a symbiotic relationship. Your expertise meets their needs, and in turn, their challenges become opportunities for you to excel. Remember, your consultancy isn't just about what you offer—it's about the transformative impact you make on the clients you serve.

Carving Your Path with Precision

In the world of consulting, defining your expertise and finding your ideal client isn't just about narrowing your focus—it's about honing in on a pathway that leads to impactful and meaningful work. As we conclude this chapter, remember that your journey is marked by the synergy between what you offer and who you serve.

Identifying your expertise gives you the power to create solutions that stem from your unique strengths and experiences. It's the compass that guides your consultancy's direction and sets you apart in a crowded market. By understanding your passion and aligning it with your skills, you're creating a space where your brilliance can flourish.

Similarly, discovering your ideal client is a dance between empathy and strategic targeting. It's about recognizing the pain points, aspirations, and needs of those who can benefit most from your expertise. Building a deep connection with your ideal client transforms your consultancy from a service provider to a trusted partner.

As you move forward, remember that the process of defining your expertise and finding your ideal client is dynamic. Just as your expertise evolves, so too do the needs of your audience. Stay attuned to these shifts, adapting your strategies to cater to an ever-changing landscape.

With your expertise as your guiding light and your ideal client as your muse, you're poised to carve a path that's uniquely yours—one that resonates with authenticity, purpose, and impact. The foundation you're building is strong, and in the chapters ahead, we'll continue to build upon it, transforming your consultancy from a concept into a thriving reality.

Chapter 3: Crafting Your Business Foundation - Objectives

In Chapter 3, our focus shifts to crafting a solid business foundation that aligns with your expertise and resonates with your ideal clients. By the end of this chapter, you will:

Formulate a Clear Consulting Business Model:

- Understand the components of a consulting business model.
- Create a framework that outlines your services, pricing, and value proposition.
- Define how your expertise and solutions uniquely address your ideal client's needs.

Build a Comprehensive Business Plan:

- Identify and articulate your consultancy's short-term and long-term goals.
- Develop a roadmap that outlines your strategies for growth, client acquisition, and service expansion.
- Explore potential challenges and devise contingency plans to address them.
- Lay the Groundwork for Brand Identity:

- Define your consultancy's brand identity, encompassing values, mission, and voice.
- Explore design elements such as logo, colors, and imagery that reflect your brand essence.
- Craft a compelling brand story that resonates with your target audience and communicates your expertise.

Establish Effective Communication Channels:

- Identify the most relevant communication channels to reach your ideal clients.
- Develop a strategy for online and offline presence, including website, social media, and networking events.
- Lay the groundwork for a content strategy that showcases your expertise and engages your audience.

Understand Legal and Financial Considerations:

- Gain insights into legal requirements and considerations for consulting businesses.
- Understand the financial aspects, including budgeting, pricing strategies, and financial projections.
- Create a plan for managing finances, taxes, and potential legal hurdles.

By achieving these objectives, you will be equipped with a well-structured business foundation that not only showcases your expertise but also aligns seamlessly with the needs and expectations of your ideal clients. Your consultancy will be poised for growth, impact, and long-term success.

Objective 1: Formulate a Clear Consulting Business Model

A robust consulting business model serves as the blueprint for your venture's success. It's the framework that defines how your expertise translates into value for your clients. Achieving this objective involves:

Understanding the Components: Delve into the key components of a consulting business model. This includes identifying your core services, pricing structure, revenue streams, and potential value-added offerings.

Defining Your Value Proposition: Your expertise is your unique selling point. Articulate how your skills, knowledge, and solutions directly address the pain points of your ideal clients. Clearly communicate the benefits they will gain by working with you.

Segmenting Your Services: Divide your offerings into packages or tiers that cater to different client needs and budgets. This segmentation enhances client choice and makes your services more accessible to a broader audience.

Objective 2: Build a Comprehensive Business Plan

A well-constructed business plan is your roadmap to success. It outlines your consultancy's goals, strategies, and contingencies. Achieving this objective entails:

Setting SMART Goals: Define Specific, Measurable, Achievable, Relevant, and Time-bound goals for your consultancy. These goals provide direction and serve as benchmarks for progress.

Developing Strategies: Lay out strategies for client acquisition, marketing, branding, and service expansion. Consider how you will reach your target audience, promote your expertise, and adapt to changing market dynamics.

Addressing Challenges: Anticipate potential challenges and setbacks your consultancy might face. Develop contingency plans to mitigate risks and ensure smooth operation even in adverse scenarios.

Objective 3: Lay the Groundwork for Brand Identity

Your brand identity is a reflection of your consultancy's personality. It's how you communicate your values and establish a connection with your clients. Achieving this objective involves:

Defining Your Brand Elements: Clearly articulate your consultancy's mission, values, and guiding principles. This foundation provides a sense of purpose and authenticity to your brand.

Visual Identity: Explore design elements that capture your brand essence. Develop a logo, color palette, and visual assets that resonate with your ideal clients and reflect your expertise.

Crafting a Compelling Story: Storytelling humanizes your brand. Develop a narrative that communicates your journey, passion, and commitment to solving client problems through your expertise.

Objective 4: Establish Effective Communication Channels

In the digital age, effective communication channels are essential for connecting with your audience. Achieving this objective entails:

Choosing Relevant Channels: Identify the communication channels where your ideal clients are most active. This could include social media platforms, industry forums, webinars, workshops, and networking events.

Developing an Online Presence: Create a professional and user-friendly website that showcases your expertise, services, and client success stories. Optimize your website for search engines to increase visibility.

Content Strategy: Craft a content strategy that demonstrates your expertise. Regularly publish blog posts, articles, videos, or podcasts that provide valuable insights to your target audience.

Objective 5: Understand Legal and Financial Considerations

Navigating legal and financial aspects is crucial for a successful consultancy. Achieving this objective involves:

Legal Requirements: Understand the legal structures available for your consultancy (e.g., sole proprietorship, LLC). Register your business, obtain necessary licenses, and ensure compliance with local regulations.

Financial Planning: Develop a comprehensive financial plan that includes budgeting, projected revenues, and expenses. Determine your pricing strategy based on your expertise, market demand, and cost of delivering services.

Risk Management: Plan for potential financial and legal challenges. Consider business insurance to protect against liability and unforeseen events that could impact your consultancy.

By extensively addressing each of these objectives, you'll be laying a strong foundation for your consultancy. This foundation is more than just a formality; it's the bedrock upon which your success will be built. With a clear business model, comprehensive plan, compelling brand, effective communication, and a grasp of legal and financial considerations, you're positioning your consultancy for growth, impact, and sustainable success in the consulting arena.

A Foundation for Success

As we wrap up Chapter 3, you've embarked on the journey of crafting a robust business foundation for your consulting venture. The objectives you've explored—formulating a clear consulting business model, building a comprehensive business plan, establishing brand identity, creating effective communication channels, and understanding legal and financial considerations—are the cornerstones upon which your consultancy's success will be built.

Your expertise, combined with a well-defined business model, ensures that the value you offer aligns seamlessly with the needs of your ideal clients. Your comprehensive business plan charts the course for growth, positioning you to overcome challenges and seize opportunities as you navigate the consultancy landscape.

With a thoughtfully developed brand identity, you're not just offering services; you're creating a connection with your audience based on shared values and aspirations. Effective communication channels amplify your reach, enabling you to showcase your expertise, engage your target audience, and provide valuable insights.

Understanding legal and financial considerations safeguards your consultancy's integrity and stability. By laying the groundwork for compliance and financial planning, you're building a solid platform for long-term success.

As you move forward, remember that the business foundation you're constructing is not static. It's a living framework that will evolve as your expertise deepens, as market dynamics change, and as you continue to refine your strategies. The effort you invest in crafting this foundation is an investment in your consultancy's future—one that's poised for growth, impact, and fulfillment.

In the upcoming chapters, we'll continue to build upon this foundation, exploring strategies to connect with your audience, deliver exceptional value, navigate challenges, and scale your consultancy. Your journey as a consulting entrepreneur is progressing, and each step you take brings you closer to transforming your vision into a thriving reality.

Chapter 4: Connecting and Engaging - Objectives

In Chapter 4, the focus shifts to establishing meaningful connections with your audience and creating engagement that resonates. By the end of this chapter, you will:

Master the Art of Effective Networking:

- Learn techniques to build genuine relationships with peers, mentors, and potential clients.
- Explore networking events, conferences, and online platforms to expand your professional circle.
- Develop strategies to make lasting impressions and leverage connections for growth.

Craft Compelling Content:

- Understand the principles of content marketing and its role in showcasing your expertise.
- Create valuable and relevant content that educates, informs, and resonates with your target audience.

- Develop a content calendar and distribution strategy for consistent engagement.

Engage Through social media:

- Utilize social media platforms to amplify your reach and connect with your audience.
- Develop a social media strategy that aligns with your brand voice and values.
- Cultivate an engaged community through interactive content, conversations, and responding to comments.

Deliver Impactful Presentations:

- Master the art of delivering compelling presentations that captivate and educate your audience.
- Learn techniques to overcome nervousness and stage fright while presenting.
- Tailor your presentations to meet the needs and expectations of your ideal clients.

Harness the Power of Webinars and Workshops:

- Understand the benefits of hosting webinars and workshops to showcase your expertise.
- Plan, promote, and execute engaging webinars and workshops that provide value to participants.

- Utilize interactive elements to encourage participation and facilitate meaningful discussions.

Leverage Thought Leadership:

- Position yourself as a thought leader in your field through consistent, insightful contributions.
- Explore opportunities to share your expertise through guest blogging, podcast appearances, or media interviews.
- Build credibility and gain visibility by offering perspectives that shape industry conversations.

By achieving these objectives, you will develop the skills and strategies necessary to establish meaningful connections, engage your audience, and showcase your expertise in ways that resonate deeply. Your consultancy's presence will be felt and valued, setting the stage for lasting relationships and impactful engagement.

Objective 1: Master the Art of Effective Networking

Master the Art of Effective Networking

Effective networking is more than just a buzzword; it's a skill that can significantly impact your personal and professional life. It's the art of building and nurturing meaningful relationships that go beyond superficial connections. In today's interconnected world, mastering this art is not just an option; it's a necessity for success. Let's delve into the nuances of effective networking and how it can elevate your life and career

Understanding Effective Networking

At its core, effective networking is about creating and maintaining a web of connections based on mutual trust, respect, and shared interests. It's not a one-time event but an ongoing process that can open doors, create opportunities, and enrich your life in various ways.

The Benefits of Effective Networking

Opportunities Abound: Effective networking introduces you to a diverse range of people, each with their own set of skills, knowledge, and connections. This exposure can lead to job opportunities, partnerships, or collaborations you might never have encountered otherwise.

Knowledge Sharing: Networking allows you to tap into the expertise of others. Whether you need advice on a specific project, insights into a particular industry, or recommendations for personal growth, your network can provide valuable information and guidance.

Boosted Confidence: As you build your network and engage in conversations, your confidence grows. This newfound self-assuredness can positively impact your career, enabling you to take on new challenges and pursue your goals more ambitiously.

Personal Growth: Networking isn't just about what you can gain; it's also about what you can give. Sharing your knowledge and experiences with others can be incredibly fulfilling and contribute to your personal growth.

The Components of Effective Networking

Effective networking isn't a one-size-fits-all concept; it's a personalized journey that evolves over time. Here are key components to consider:

1. **Authenticity**: Be genuine and authentic in your interactions. People are more likely to connect with someone who is sincere and transparent.

2. **Listening Skills**: Effective networking involves active listening. Pay attention to what others are saying, ask questions, and show a genuine interest in their perspectives.

3. **Value Exchange**: Networking is a two-way street. Offer help, advice, or resources to your connections as much as you seek assistance from them.

4. **Diversity**: Cultivate a diverse network that includes individuals from various backgrounds, industries, and professions. Diverse perspectives can lead to fresh ideas and innovative solutions.

5. **Consistency**: Networking isn't something you do once and forget. It requires ongoing effort. Regularly nurture your connections by staying in touch and showing appreciation.

Building Your Networking Skills

Networking skills can be honed and improved over time. Here are some practical steps to help you master the art of effective networking:

- **Set Clear Goals**: Determine what you hope to achieve through networking. Are you looking for career opportunities, mentors, or industry insights? Clear goals will guide your networking efforts.

- **Attend Events**: Attend industry conferences, seminars, workshops, and social gatherings to meet like-minded individuals. These events provide excellent networking opportunities.

- **Online Presence**: Utilize social media platforms like LinkedIn to connect with professionals in your field. Share valuable content and engage in discussions to expand your network.

- **Follow Up:** After meeting someone new, follow up with a personalized message or email. Express your gratitude for the connection and suggest a potential way to collaborate or stay in touch.

- **Join Groups or Associations**: Consider joining professional associations or interest groups related to your field. These organizations often host networking events and offer valuable resources.

- **Practice Elevator Pitches:** Be prepared to introduce yourself succinctly and confidently. An elevator pitch should convey who you are, what you do, and what you're passionate about.

- **Mentorship**: Seek out mentors or experienced individuals in your industry who can provide guidance and support in your professional journey.

Building Bridges with Barry:

Barry, a seasoned consultant, understood the power of networking. At a conference, he engaged in genuine conversations with fellow attendees, sharing insights and listening to their challenges. One such conversation led to a collaboration with another consultant. They combined their expertise to offer a comprehensive solution that neither could have provided alone. Barry's willingness to connect and collaborate transformed a chance encounter into a strategic partnership.

The Endless Possibilities of Networking

Effective networking is not merely a skill; it's a mindset that opens doors to countless possibilities. It's a continuous process of building relationships, sharing knowledge, and growing both personally and professionally.

As you master the art of effective networking, you'll find that the connections you cultivate can enrich your life in ways you may never have imagined. Whether you're pursuing career advancement, seeking personal growth, or striving for entrepreneurial success, your network can be your most valuable asset on your journey.

So, go ahead, embark on this networking adventure, and watch the world of opportunities unfold before you.

Objective 2: Crafting Compelling Content

Crafting compelling content is both an art and a science. Whether you're writing an article, a blog post, a social media update, or any other form of content, the goal is to capture your audience's attention, keep them engaged, and convey your message effectively. Here's a step-by-step guide to help you craft compelling content:

1. Know Your Audience:

Understand your target audience's demographics, interests, and pain points.

Create buyer personas to represent your ideal readers or customers.

Tailor your content to address their specific needs and preferences.

2. Define Your Purpose:

Clarify the purpose of your content. Are you informing, entertaining, inspiring, or persuading?

Have a clear call to action (CTA) in mind. What do you want your audience to do after engaging with your content?

3. Research Thoroughly:

Gather relevant information and data to support your content.

Cite credible sources to enhance your content's credibility.

Use keyword research to optimize your content for search engines if applicable.

4. Craft a Captivating Headline:

Your headline is the first thing readers see. Make it attention-grabbing and relevant.

Use power words, numbers, and curiosity to pique interest.

Promise value or a solution to the reader's problem.

5. Create an Engaging Introduction:

Your introduction should set the tone and provide context for your content.

Pose a question, share a compelling anecdote, or present a surprising fact to draw readers in.

6. Organize Your Content:

Use clear headings and subheadings to structure your content.

Break up long paragraphs into shorter, digestible chunks.

Use bullet points and numbered lists for easy scanning.

7. Tell a Story:

Storytelling humanizes your content and creates an emotional connection.

Use narratives, case studies, or personal experiences to illustrate your points.

Make your audience the hero of the story.

8. Be Concise and Clear:

Avoid jargon and overly complex language.

Use simple, concise sentences to convey your message.

Eliminate unnecessary words and redundancies.

9. **Use Visuals**:

Incorporate images, infographics, videos, and other visual elements to enhance your content.

Visuals break up text and make content more appealing.

10. **Provide Value**:

- Offer valuable insights, solutions, or information that addresses your audience's needs.

- Solve a problem or answer a question your readers might have.

11. **Use Persuasive Language**:

- Use persuasive techniques like storytelling, testimonials, and social proof to influence your audience.

- Highlight benefits and show how your content benefits the reader.

12. **Encourage Engagement**:

- Include a clear CTA that tells readers what to do next.

- Invite comments, questions, or social shares to foster interaction.

13. Proofread and Edit:

- Review your content for grammar, spelling, and punctuation errors.

- Ensure consistency in style and tone throughout your content.

14. Test and Iterate:

- Analyze the performance of your content using analytics tools.

- Pay attention to metrics like engagement, click-through rates, and conversion rates.

- Use the insights to refine and improve future content.

15. Be Authentic:

- Write in your own voice and be authentic in your communication.

- Show your personality and connect with your audience on a human level.

Crafting compelling content is an ongoing process of learning and refinement. It's about delivering value, resonating with your audience, and creating content that leaves a lasting impact. By following these steps and continually adapting to your audience's feedback, you'll become a master at crafting content that captivates and converts.

Amy's Blogging Journey:

Amy, a consultant specializing in productivity, started a blog sharing tips and strategies. Her blog posts provided actionable advice that resonated with her audience. Over time, her blog gained traction, attracting readers seeking solutions to their productivity woes. This consistent content creation not only established Amy as an expert in her field but also became a valuable resource that attracted potential clients.

Objective 3: Engage Through social media

Engaging through social media is a powerful way to connect with your audience, build brand awareness, and foster meaningful relationships. Whether you're using social media for personal branding, marketing your business, or simply looking to connect with like-minded individuals, here's a comprehensive guide to help you effectively engage through social media:

1. **Know Your Audience**:

Understand your target audience's demographics, interests, and behaviors.

Create detailed buyer personas to represent your ideal social media followers.

Tailor your content to resonate with your audience's preferences and pain points.

2. **Choose the Right Platforms**:

Focus your efforts on the social media platforms that align with your audience's demographics and interests.

Different platforms serve different purposes, so select the ones that best suit your goals.

3. **Create High-Quality Content**:

Craft visually appealing and informative content that provides value to your audience.

Use a mix of content types, including text, images, videos, infographics, and stories.

Ensure your content is consistent with your brand's voice and style.

4. Post Consistently:

Establish a regular posting schedule to keep your audience engaged.

Consistency helps maintain your brand presence and keeps your followers informed.

5. Encourage Two-Way Communication:

Respond promptly to comments, messages, and mentions. Engage in conversations.

Show appreciation for positive feedback and address concerns or criticisms constructively.

6. Use Hashtags Wisely:

Research and use relevant hashtags to increase the discoverability of your content.

Avoid overusing hashtags, as it can make your posts appear spammy.

7. Leverage User-Generated Content (UGC):

Encourage your followers to create and share content related to your brand or products.

Repost UGC to showcase authentic experiences and build trust.

8. Host Contests and Giveaways:

Organize fun and interactive contests or giveaways to boost engagement.

Ensure the rules and prizes are clear, and promote the event effectively.

9. Share Valuable Insights:

Offer informative and educational content that addresses your audience's questions or interests.

Share industry trends, tips, and how-to guides to establish your expertise.

10. Live Video and Stories:

- Use live video on platforms like Instagram and Facebook to connect with your audience in real-time.

- Share behind-the-scenes moments, host Q&A sessions, or showcase product launches.

11. Collaborate and Partner:

- Collaborate with influencers or complementary businesses to expand your reach.

- Partnering can introduce your brand to new audiences and create engaging content.

12. Analyze and Adapt:

- Use social media analytics tools to measure the performance of your content and campaigns.

- Track engagement metrics, such as likes, comments, shares, and click-through rates.

- Use the insights to refine your social media strategy and improve engagement over time.

13. Be Authentic:

- Be yourself on social media. Authenticity builds trust and fosters stronger connections.

- Share personal stories, experiences, and a genuine passion for your subject matter.

14. Stay Updated:

- Keep up with social media trends and algorithm changes.

- Experiment with new features and formats as they become available.

15. Monitor Your Online Reputation:

- Regularly monitor what's being said about your brand online.

- Address any negative feedback or reviews professionally and constructively.

Engaging through social media is an ongoing process that requires dedication and a genuine interest in connecting with your audience. By consistently delivering valuable content, fostering interactions, and adapting to the evolving social media landscape, you can build a loyal following and achieve your engagement goals.

Jake's Engaging Conversations:

Jake, a marketing consultant, used social media to foster engagement. He posed thought-provoking questions, shared industry insights, and responded to comments with genuine interest. By engaging in meaningful conversations, he cultivated a community that valued his expertise. This engagement translated into loyal followers who later turned to him for consulting services, knowing he truly understood their needs.

Objective 4: Deliver Impactful Presentations

Delivering impactful presentations is a valuable skill that can greatly influence your success in various areas, whether it's in your career, education, or public speaking engagements. Here's a comprehensive guide to help you deliver presentations that captivate your audience and leave a lasting impact:

1. **Understand Your Audience**:

Know your audience's demographics, interests, and knowledge level.

Tailor your content and approach to resonate with your specific audience.

2. Define Clear Objectives:

Clarify the purpose of your presentation. What do you want to achieve?

Set clear, measurable objectives that guide your content and delivery.

3. Organize Your Content:

Structure your presentation logically with a clear beginning, middle, and end.

Use a compelling opening to grab your audience's attention.

Present your main points in a coherent sequence.

4. Engaging Opening

Start with a story, a relevant quote, a surprising fact, or a compelling question.

An engaging opening sets the tone and piques your audience's interest.

5. Visual Aids:

Use visuals like slides, images, and videos to complement your message.

Keep slides clean and uncluttered, focusing on key points.

6. Rehearse Regularly

Rehearse your presentation multiple times to become comfortable with the content.

Practice in front of a mirror, record yourself, or present to a trusted friend for feedback.

7. **Use Your Voice Effectively**:

Vary your tone, pitch, and pace to maintain audience engagement.

Speak clearly and confidently, projecting your voice to ensure everyone can hear.

8. **Body Language**:

Maintain good posture, stand or sit confidently, and avoid distracting movements.

Use gestures purposefully to emphasize points and connect with your audience.

9. **Interaction and Engagement**:

Encourage audience participation through questions, polls, or discussions.

Foster a sense of involvement rather than passive listening.

10. **Storytelling**:

- Weave relevant stories into your presentation to illustrate key points.

- Stories create an emotional connection and make information memorable.

11. Be Concise:

- Avoid information overload. Focus on the most important and relevant content.

- Less is often more; clarity is key.

12. Use Analogies and Examples:

- Analogies and examples simplify complex concepts and make them relatable.

- They help your audience grasp and remember your message.

13. Handling Q&A:

- Prepare for potential questions and challenges.

- Respond to questions with confidence, and admit if you don't know the answer, offering to follow up.

14. Practice Empathy:

- Understand your audience's perspective and concerns.

- Address their needs and concerns in your presentation.

15. Summarize and Conclude:

- Summarize the main points of your presentation to reinforce key takeaways.

- End with a strong and memorable closing statement or call to action.

16. **Seek Feedback**:

- After your presentation, solicit feedback from your audience or colleagues.

- Use feedback to continuously improve your presentation skills.

17. **Manage Nervousness**:

- Accept that some nervousness is normal. Channel it into energy and enthusiasm.

- Techniques like deep breathing and mindfulness can help manage anxiety.

18. **Visualize Success**:

- Visualize a successful presentation in your mind before you begin.

- Positive visualization can boost your confidence and performance.

19. **Record Yourself**:

- Record your presentations to review your performance objectively.

- Identify areas for improvement in both content and delivery.

20. **Continuous Improvement**:

- Keep learning and growing as a presenter.

- Attend workshops, read books, and watch masterful speakers to refine your skills.

Delivering impactful presentations is a skill that can be developed and refined over time. With practice, preparation, and a focus on connecting with your audience, you can become a confident and influential presenter, leaving a lasting impact on your audience.

Samantha's Unforgettable Workshop:

Samantha, an HR consultant, conducted a workshop on employee engagement. Instead of a traditional lecture, she incorporated group discussions and interactive exercises. Participants felt involved and left with actionable takeaways. Months later, a participant reached out to Samantha to hire her for a consultation, highlighting how her engaging presentation left a lasting impression.

Connecting and Engaging for Lasting Impact

As we conclude Chapter 4, you've embarked on a journey of building connections and creating engagement that leaves a lasting mark. The objectives you've explored—mastering networking, crafting compelling content, engaging through social media, delivering impactful presentations, harnessing webinars and workshops, and leveraging thought leadership—underscore the significance of building relationships and showcasing your expertise.

In a world driven by connections, your ability to authentically network opens doors to collaborations, partnerships, and opportunities you might not have envisioned. Crafting compelling content not only educates your audience but also establishes you as a go-to resource, contributing to your consultancy's growth.

Engaging through social media creates a space for dialogue, enabling you to connect with your audience on a personal level. Effective presentations and workshops captivate your audience, leaving them with insights that resonate long after the session ends. Webinars provide a platform to showcase your expertise in real-time, while thought leadership elevates your status as a respected industry voice.

Remember that each interaction is a chance to create a connection, each piece of content is an opportunity to educate, and each presentation is a platform to captivate your audience. The relationships you build, the knowledge you share, and the engagement you foster contribute to your consultancy's reputation and impact.

As you continue your journey, keep in mind that the connections you cultivate and the engagement you create are not just transactional—they're the bedrock of meaningful relationships that will shape your consultancy's success. In the chapters ahead, we'll delve deeper into strategies for delivering exceptional value, navigating challenges, and scaling your consultancy while maintaining the connections you've nurtured. Your path is illuminated, and every step you take brings you closer to the pinnacle of consulting excellence.

Chapter 5: Delivering Value and Navigating Challenges

In Chapter 5, the focus shifts to the core of your consultancy—delivering exceptional value to clients and navigating challenges with finesse. By the end of this chapter, you will

Master the Art of Client-Centric Approach:

- Understand the importance of tailoring your services to meet the unique needs of each client.
- Develop strategies for effective client communication, active listening, and building trust.
- Create a seamless client experience that fosters long-term relationships.

Provide Solutions, Not Just Services:

- Shift from transactional service delivery to offering holistic solutions that address underlying issues.
- Explore techniques for analyzing client pain points, diagnosing challenges, and proposing comprehensive strategies.

Overcome Client Objections and Concerns:

- Identify common objections clients may raise and develop effective responses.

- Learn to navigate objections with empathy and provide insights that alleviate concerns.

Navigate Difficult Client Situations:

- Gain strategies for managing challenging client interactions with professionalism and grace.
- Develop conflict resolution skills that preserve client relationships and project integrity.

Adapt to Changing Client Needs and Expectations:

- Stay attuned to evolving client needs and industry trends.
- Develop the flexibility to adjust your services and strategies to align with changing expectations.

Manage Time and Scope Effectively:

- Understand the importance of time management and maintaining project scope.
- Learn techniques for setting realistic expectations, managing deadlines, and preventing scope creep.

By achieving these objectives, you will not only enhance your consultancy's reputation but also strengthen your ability to deliver value that makes a lasting impact. Navigating challenges with professionalism and adaptability ensures your consultancy's resilience and sustained success.

Objective 1: Master the Art of Client-Centric Approach

This objective centers on placing your clients at the heart of your consultancy. It involves understanding their unique needs, building strong relationships, and creating an experience that leaves a positive and lasting impression. To achieve this objective:

Tailoring Services: Recognize that each client is distinct. Customize your services to match their specific challenges, goals, and preferences.

Effective Communication: Foster open lines of communication by actively listening to clients. Understand their concerns, questions, and aspirations.

Building Trust: Establish a foundation of trust by delivering on promises, being transparent, and demonstrating your expertise.

Client Experience: Create a seamless and memorable journey for clients—from the initial interaction to the project's conclusion. The overall experience matters as much as the results.

Objective 2: Provide Solutions, Not Just Services

Moving beyond transactional interactions, this objective emphasizes delivering comprehensive solutions that address the root causes of clients' challenges. Achieve this by:

Analyzing Pain Points: Dig deep into clients' pain points and challenges to uncover underlying issues. This requires asking probing questions and gaining a holistic understanding.

Diagnosing Challenges: Apply your expertise to diagnose the root causes of problems. This enables you to offer strategic solutions that lead to sustainable improvements.

Holistic Strategies: Develop strategies that encompass various aspects of a challenge. Show clients how each element contributes to the overall solution.

Objective 3: Overcome Client Objections and Concerns

Client objections are common, and effectively addressing them builds trust and credibility. To succeed in this objective:

Identify Objections: Anticipate objections clients might raise regarding your services, pricing, or approach.

Empathetic Responses: Respond to objections with empathy and understanding. Address concerns while highlighting the value you offer.

Value Communication: Articulate the value clients gain from working with you. Show how your solutions outweigh their objections.

Objective 4: Navigate Difficult Client Situations

Challenging client interactions require finesse and professionalism. To navigate these situations effectively:

Professionalism: Approach difficult conversations with a calm and professional demeanor. Maintain respect even when facing disagreements.

Conflict Resolution: Develop skills to de-escalate conflicts and find mutually beneficial solutions. Focus on preserving the client relationship.

Project Integrity: Ensure that challenges don't compromise the integrity of your project or your consultancy's reputation.

Objective 5: Adapt to Changing Client Needs and Expectations

In a dynamic business environment, client needs and expectations evolve. To stay relevant:

Market Awareness: Stay updated on industry trends, shifts, and emerging needs.

Flexibility: Adapt your strategies and offerings to align with changing client expectations.

Proactive Approach: Anticipate shifts and proactively offer solutions that cater to evolving demands.

Objective 6: Manage Time and Scope Effectively

Effective time and scope management ensure projects stay on track and expectations are met. To excel in this area:

Time Management: Set realistic timelines and deadlines. Communicate clearly about project phases, timelines, and expectations.

Scope Definition: Clearly outline the scope of your services to avoid scope creep. Preventing scope creep maintains project focus and client satisfaction.

By achieving these objectives, you're equipping yourself with the skills and strategies needed to not only deliver value that meets client needs but also improving the chances of your business being a success.

Delivering Value and Navigating Challenges with Excellence

As we wrap up Chapter 5, you've delved into the core of consultancy—delivering unparalleled value and navigating challenges with finesse. The objectives you've explored—mastering a client-centric approach, providing holistic solutions, overcoming objections, managing difficult situations, adapting to changing needs, and effective time and scope management—underscore the essence of being a trusted consultant.

Mastering a client-centric approach isn't just about delivering services—it's about understanding and addressing the unique needs of each client. Providing solutions, not just services, sets you apart by uncovering underlying issues and delivering transformative results.

Overcoming objections and navigating challenging situations with grace builds credibility and strengthens relationships. Adapting to changing client needs and expectations showcases your agility and commitment to meeting evolving demands. Effective time and scope management ensures that your projects are not only successful but also aligned with client expectations.

As you proceed in your consulting journey, remember that the value you provide and the challenges you navigate are markers of your expertise and professionalism. Each client interaction, solution delivered, and challenge overcome is a testament to your dedication to making a positive impact.

In the chapters ahead, we'll continue to explore strategies for scaling your consultancy, honing your leadership skills, and achieving sustained success. The foundation you've laid through delivering value and navigating challenges positions you for growth, influence, and continued excellence in the world of consultancy.

Chapter 6: Scaling Your Consultancy and Leading with Impact

In Chapter 6, we embark on a transformative journey—one that takes your consultancy to new heights and equips you with leadership skills to lead with impact. As you delve into this chapter, you'll explore a series of objectives designed to guide you through the process of scaling your consultancy and becoming a influential leader in your field.

Objectives:

Develop a Scalability Strategy:

- Understand the principles of scalability and its relevance to your consultancy's growth.
- Explore different paths to scale, whether through expanding services, entering new markets, or forming strategic partnerships.
- Create a detailed plan that outlines your approach, resources required, and potential challenges.

Build a High-Performing Team:

- Recognize the importance of assembling a team that complements your expertise.
- Learn strategies for effective team building, from hiring the right talent to fostering a collaborative culture.
- Develop leadership skills that empower your team members and encourage their professional growth.

Cultivate Thought Leadership:

- Elevate your influence by positioning yourself as a thought leader in your industry.
- Develop strategies for consistently sharing valuable insights through content creation, speaking engagements, and industry contributions.
- Leverage your thought leadership to attract high-profile clients and establish credibility.

Lead with Impact:

- Embrace the role of a leader within your consultancy and industry.
- Develop a leadership style that aligns with your values and vision, fostering trust and respect.
- Inspire and motivate your team, clients, and peers through clear communication and visionary guidance.

Implement Effective Processes and Systems:

- Recognize the significance of streamlined processes and systems in supporting scalability.

- Explore tools and technologies that enhance efficiency, from project management software to CRM systems.
- Implement processes that ensure consistent service delivery, client communication, and project management.

Foster Continuous Improvement:

- Embrace a mindset of ongoing learning and improvement for yourself and your consultancy.
- Encourage a culture of innovation and adaptability within your team.
- Continuously seek feedback from clients, team members, and peers to refine your offerings and strategies.

As you embark on this chapter, each objective becomes a stepping stone toward achieving a consultancy that's not only successful but also influential.

By scaling your consultancy, building a high-performing team, cultivating thought leadership, leading with impact, implementing effective processes, and fostering continuous improvement, you're setting the stage for sustained growth, transformative leadership, and a consultancy that leaves a lasting legacy in your industry.

Objective 1: Develop a Scalability Strategy

Scaling your consultancy involves strategic expansion while maintaining the quality of your services. This objective centers on understanding the principles of scalability and crafting a well-defined strategy that paves the way for growth. Here's a breakdown:

Understanding Scalability: Recognize that scalability isn't just about growth in size; it's about expanding your consultancy's reach, impact, and revenue without sacrificing quality. It's a balance between growth and maintaining the value you provide to clients.

Exploring Paths to Scale: Consider various approaches to scale your consultancy. This could involve diversifying your services to cater to a broader audience, entering new markets or industries, or forming strategic partnerships that complement your expertise.

Creating a Detailed Plan: Outline a comprehensive strategy that outlines the steps, resources, and timeline required for scalability. Identify potential challenges and develop contingency plans to address them effectively.

Resource Allocation: Assess the resources—financial, human, and technological—required to execute your scalability strategy. Ensure you have the necessary resources to support the expansion.

Adaptability: Recognize that a scalability strategy isn't static. It should be adaptable to changing market conditions, client needs, and industry trends.

Navigating New Horizons: Sarah's Journey to Consultancy Expansion

Sarah, a business consultant, recognized the growing demand for her services. She decided to scale her consultancy by expanding into new markets. She researched different industries and identified a niche where her expertise could add significant value. Sarah developed a detailed plan that included market research, marketing strategies, and collaborations with local businesses. She understood the importance of allocating resources effectively to support her expansion. Sarah's scalability strategy not only led to increased revenue but also positioned her as a leader in her chosen niche.

By understanding scalability and developing a clear strategy, you're setting the foundation for sustainable growth that allows your consultancy to reach new heights while maintaining the quality and value that define your expertise.

Objective 2: Build a High-Performing Team

Building a High-Performing Team

In the world of consultancy, the strength of your team can make all the difference. A high-performing team isn't just a group of individuals working together; it's a collective force capable of achieving exceptional results. Whether you're a seasoned consultancy leader or just starting out, understanding the key principles of team building is essential for success.

1. **Clear Vision and Purpose:**

To build a high-performing team, start with a clear and compelling vision. Your team members need to understand the overall goal and the purpose behind their work. This clarity provides direction and motivation, aligning everyone toward a common objective. It's not just about what you do but why you do it.

2. **Diverse Skill Sets**:

Effective teams often comprise individuals with diverse skills and expertise. Embrace this diversity; it can be a source of innovation and creativity. A team with a range of talents can tackle complex challenges more comprehensively.

3. **Strong Leadership**:

Leadership sets the tone for the team. A strong leader provides guidance, support, and inspiration. They foster an environment of trust and open communication, encouraging team members to contribute their best.

4. **Effective Communication**:

Open, honest, and frequent communication is the lifeblood of high-performing teams. Encourage team members to share their ideas, concerns, and feedback. Effective communication ensures that everyone is on the same page and can address issues proactively.

5. **Collaboration and Trust**:

Trust is the foundation of any successful team. Foster an environment where team members trust each other's competence and intentions. Encourage collaboration by emphasizing that everyone's input is valued.

6. **Clearly Defined Roles and Responsibilities**:

Each team member should have a well-defined role and understand their responsibilities. This prevents duplication of effort and ensures that everyone knows what's expected of them.

7. **Recognition and Appreciation**:

Recognize and appreciate your team members' contributions. Acknowledgment and praise can go a long way in motivating and retaining top talent.

8. **Continuous Learning and Development**:

Invest in your team's growth. Provide opportunities for training and development, keeping them up-to-date with industry trends and enhancing their skills.

9. **Results-Oriented**:

High-performing teams focus on results. Set measurable goals and track progress regularly. Celebrate achievements and learn from setbacks.

10. **Adaptability**:

The business landscape is ever-changing. A high-performing team is adaptable and responsive to new challenges and opportunities. Encourage a culture of continuous improvement.

11. Conflict Resolution:

Conflict is natural in any team. However, the key is in how conflicts are managed. Teach your team effective conflict resolution strategies, emphasizing a focus on solutions, not blame.

12. Work-Life Balance:

Remember that your team members have lives outside of work. Encourage a healthy work-life balance to prevent burnout and maintain long-term performance.

13. Lead by Example:

As a leader, your actions set the standard. Demonstrate the qualities and behaviors you expect from your team members.

Building a high-performing team takes time and effort, but the results are well worth it. Such teams not only deliver exceptional results but also become the backbone of your consultancy's success. They're the engine that drives innovation, client satisfaction, and growth.

Invest in your team, nurture their talents, and provide them with the tools and environment they need to excel. In doing so, you'll not only build a consultancy that thrives but also create a fulfilling professional journey for yourself and those you lead.

Synergizing Success: Mark's Team-Driven Consultancy Expansion

Mark, a marketing consultant, realized that to expand his consultancy, he needed a team with diverse skills. He hired specialists in social media, content creation, and data analysis. Mark focused on creating a collaborative culture by holding regular team meetings, where members shared insights and learned from one another. He empowered his team to take ownership of projects and make decisions in their respective domains. This approach not only led to improved project outcomes but also encouraged team members to contribute innovative ideas that enhanced the consultancy's services.

By building a high-performing team that aligns with your consultancy's values and goals, you're creating a foundation for growth and success. A cohesive and capable team enhances your consultancy's capacity to take on larger projects, offer more comprehensive solutions, and reach a wider audience.

Objective 3: Cultivate Thought Leadership

Positioning yourself as a thought leader in your industry elevates your consultancy's influence and credibility. This objective involves consistently sharing valuable insights, contributing to industry conversations, and leveraging your expertise to attract high-profile clients.

Here's a deeper dive:

Thought Leadership Defined: Understand that thought leadership goes beyond expertise—it's about being at the forefront of industry trends, leading discussions, and shaping perspectives.

Valuable Insights: Regularly share insights that offer unique perspectives, solve industry challenges, and provide actionable advice. Your contributions should enrich the knowledge of your peers and clients.

Content Creation: Develop a content strategy that includes blog posts, articles, whitepapers, videos, or podcasts. Share your expertise on platforms where your target audience is active.

Speaking Engagements: Look for opportunities to speak at industry conferences, webinars, workshops, and events.

Present your expertise in a way that resonates with your audience.

Industry Contributions: Participate in discussions on social media, industry forums, and publications. Engage in conversations that showcase your expertise and provide value to the community.

Eco Trailblazer: Emily's Journey to Sustainable Thought Leadership

Emily, a sustainability consultant, recognized the need to position herself as a thought leader in her field. She started by consistently publishing insightful articles on sustainable practices, which gained traction within her industry. Emily also participated in webinars and panel discussions, where she shared her expertise on sustainable business strategies. Her thought leadership not only attracted attention from high-profile clients seeking her guidance but also led to invitations to speak at prominent sustainability conferences.

By cultivating thought leadership, you're establishing yourself as an authority in your industry. This not only enhances your consultancy's reputation but also attracts clients who value your expertise and insights. Thought leadership is a powerful tool that positions you as a trusted advisor and opens doors to new opportunities and collaborations.

Objective 4: Lead with Impact

Stepping into a leadership role within your consultancy and industry is pivotal for driving growth and making a lasting impact. This objective involves developing a leadership style that aligns with your values, inspiring your team, clients, and peers, and providing visionary guidance. Here's a closer look:

Embrace Leadership: Recognize that as your consultancy grows, your role as a leader becomes essential. Embrace this responsibility with enthusiasm and commitment.

Leadership Style: Develop a leadership style that reflects your values, communication preferences, and approach to decision-making. Authenticity is key to gaining trust and respect.

Inspire and Motivate: Lead by example and inspire your team to excel. Motivate them by setting clear expectations, providing mentorship, and recognizing their contributions.

Clear Communication: Communicate your vision, goals, and strategies clearly to your team and clients. Effective communication ensures everyone is aligned and working toward the same objectives.

Influence Beyond Your Team: Extend your leadership influence to the wider industry by participating in industry associations, events, and collaborations.

Tech Visionary: John's Leadership Journey in Consulting Excellence

John, a technology consultant, understood that his role as a leader was essential for guiding his consultancy's growth. He developed a leadership style that emphasized open communication and collaboration. John inspired his team by setting high standards and recognizing their achievements. His clear communication of the consultancy's vision fostered a sense of purpose and alignment. Beyond his team, John actively participated in industry conferences and discussions, sharing his insights and contributing to the growth of the field.

By leading with impact, you're creating a culture of excellence and growth within your consultancy. Your leadership style sets the tone for your team's performance, your clients' experiences, and your consultancy's overall direction. As a leader, your influence extends beyond your immediate team, shaping the industry's landscape and contributing to its progress.

Objective 5: Implement Effective Processes and Systems

Efficiency and consistency are essential as your consultancy scales. This objective revolves around implementing streamlined processes and systems that support your consultancy's growth while ensuring high-quality service delivery. Let's dive into the details:

Recognizing the Importance: Understand that efficient processes and systems are the backbone of a successful and scalable consultancy. They enhance productivity, minimize errors, and support your team's efforts.

Streamlined Operations: Identify key areas that can benefit from streamlined processes, such as client onboarding, project management, and communication.

Technology and Tools: Explore tools and technologies that enhance efficiency, such as project management software, CRM systems, and communication platforms.

Consistent Service Delivery: Implement processes that ensure consistent service delivery across different projects and clients. Consistency reinforces your consultancy's reputation for excellence.

Flexibility and Adaptation: While processes provide structure, they should also allow for flexibility to adapt to changing client needs and market dynamics.

Efficiency in Action: Lisa's Transformation in HR Consulting

Lisa, an HR consultant, realized that as her consultancy expanded, manual processes were becoming time-consuming and error-prone. She implemented a project management tool that streamlined client onboarding, task assignments, and communication. This allowed her team to collaborate more effectively and provided clients with a transparent view of project progress. Lisa's implementation of efficient processes not only improved client satisfaction but also allowed her to take on larger projects without sacrificing quality.

By implementing effective processes and systems, you're setting your consultancy up for sustained success. Streamlined operations enhance productivity and client satisfaction, while consistent service delivery establishes your consultancy as a reliable partner. As you scale, efficient processes become even more critical, enabling you to manage larger projects, serve more clients, and maintain the high standards that define your consultancy.

Objective 6: Foster Continuous Improvement

The journey of growth and success is ongoing, and continuous improvement is a mindset that keeps your consultancy ahead of the curve. This objective revolves around embracing a culture of learning, innovation, and refinement. Let's explore the details:

Commitment to Learning: Recognize that there's always room to learn and improve. Embrace a mindset of curiosity and a willingness to explore new ideas and approaches.

Innovation: Encourage your team to think creatively and explore innovative solutions to industry challenges. Embrace new technologies and methodologies that enhance your consultancy's offerings.

Feedback Loop: Create channels for feedback from clients, team members, and industry peers. Constructive feedback offers insights into areas for improvement and growth.

Adaptability: Stay flexible and open to change. Adapt your strategies, services, and processes in response to evolving client needs and market trends.

Professional Development: Invest in your own professional development and that of your team. Provide opportunities for skill enhancement, training, and industry certifications.

Financial Excellence: Michael's Journey of Continuous Improvement in Consulting

Michael, a financial consultant, believed that continuous improvement was key to staying ahead in a competitive industry. He regularly sought feedback from clients after completing projects, asking for insights into their experience and suggestions for enhancement. Michael encouraged his team to attend industry conferences and workshops to stay updated on the latest trends. He also embraced new financial technologies that improved the efficiency and accuracy of his services. Michael's dedication to continuous improvement not only boosted client satisfaction but also solidified his consultancy's reputation for innovation.

By fostering a culture of continuous improvement, you're positioning your consultancy for ongoing success. Learning from feedback, embracing innovation, and staying adaptable ensure that you're consistently delivering value that meets evolving client needs. Your commitment to growth and enhancement reinforces your consultancy's relevance and positions you as a forward-thinking leader in your industry.

A Journey of Growth, Excellence, and Impact

As we conclude Chapter 6, you've embarked on a transformative journey—one that has taken you from the foundations of consultancy to the pinnacle of leadership and influence. The objectives explored in this chapter—developing a scalability strategy, building a high-performing team, cultivating thought leadership, leading with impact, implementing effective processes and systems, and fostering continuous improvement—paint a vivid picture of the path you've traversed.

Your dedication to scaling your consultancy has set the stage for expansive growth while maintaining the quality that defines your expertise. Building a high-performing team ensures that your consultancy's impact extends beyond your individual capabilities. Cultivating thought leadership positions, you as a beacon of knowledge and insight in your industry.

Leading with impact not only elevates your consultancy but also inspires those around you to excel. Implementing efficient processes and systems enables you to deliver consistent, high-quality service. And fostering a culture of continuous improvement ensures that you're always at the forefront of innovation.

As you move forward, remember that this journey is far from over. Each objective you've pursued has equipped you with the tools, skills, and mindset to navigate the ever-evolving landscape of consultancy. Your consultancy's growth, influence, and impact are testaments to your dedication, expertise, and commitment to excellence.

In the chapters that follow, we'll delve into additional strategies for refining your leadership, overcoming unique challenges, and achieving long-term sustainability. Your consultancy's story continues, and each chapter brings you closer to the fulfillment of your vision—an enduring legacy of growth, excellence, and meaningful impact.

Chapter 7: Navigating Challenges and Ensuring Sustainability

In Chapter 7, we confront the inevitable challenges that come with consultancy and explore strategies to ensure the long-term sustainability of your practice. This chapter is a guide to overcoming obstacles, adapting to change, and building a consultancy that stands the test of time. The objectives for this chapter are as follows:

Objectives:

Identify Common Consultancy Challenges:

- Gain a comprehensive understanding of challenges that consultants often encounter.
- Learn to recognize early signs of potential challenges and risks.

Develop Resilience and Adaptability:

- Cultivate resilience in the face of adversity and unexpected obstacles.
- Embrace adaptability to navigate changing client needs and industry shifts.

Effective Problem Solving and Decision Making:

- Refine your problem-solving skills to address challenges effectively.
- Develop a structured approach to making well-informed decisions under pressure.

Mitigate Risks and Uncertainties:

- Understand the importance of risk management in maintaining consultancy sustainability.
- Learn strategies to identify, assess, and mitigate risks.

Maintain Ethical Integrity:

- Prioritize ethical considerations in every aspect of your consultancy.
- Build a reputation for ethical conduct that fosters trust and credibility.

Plan for Long-Term Sustainability:

- Develop a strategic plan that outlines your consultancy's goals for sustained success.
- Consider factors such as succession planning, growth strategies, and evolving market dynamics.

By mastering these objectives, you'll be equipped to tackle challenges head-on, adapt to changing circumstances, and build a consultancy that not only survives but thrives in an ever-evolving business landscape. Your ability to navigate challenges and ensure sustainability sets the stage for a consultancy that leaves a lasting legacy.

Objective 1: Identify Common Consultancy Challenges

This objective involves understanding the common challenges that consultants often encounter and learning to recognize early indicators of potential issues. Let's delve into the details.

Comprehensive Understanding: Take the time to familiarize yourself with the challenges that are prevalent in the consultancy industry. These challenges can range from client communication issues to project scope creep, market fluctuations, and resource constraints.

Early Recognition: Develop the ability to spot early signs of potential challenges. By identifying warning signals before they escalate, you can take proactive steps to address them and minimize their impact on your consultancy.

Client Relationship Challenges: Be aware of potential hurdles in client relationships, such as miscommunication, differing expectations, or changing client needs.

Operational Challenges: Understand operational challenges that might arise, such as resource allocation, time management, and project coordination.

Market Dynamics: Stay informed about industry trends and shifts that could impact your consultancy's operations, such as changes in demand, technological advancements, and regulatory changes.

Scope Mastery: Sarah's Solution to Navigating Project Challenges

Sarah, a marketing consultant, encountered a common challenge when one of her projects experienced scope creeps. Initially, the project seemed well-defined, but as the client's requests expanded, the project's scope became unclear. Recognizing this challenge early, Sarah engaged in open communication with the client to clarify the project's scope, objectives, and deliverables. By addressing the issue proactively, she prevented potential delays and ensured the project's successful completion.

By mastering this objective, you're equipping yourself with the ability to anticipate and address challenges before they escalate. This proactive approach enhances your consultancy's ability to navigate obstacles and maintain client satisfaction, ultimately contributing to your consultancy's sustainability and success.

Objective 2: Develop Resilience and Adaptability

This objective focuses on building the capacity to weather challenges with resilience and adaptability. It's about embracing change, bouncing back from setbacks, and thriving in the face of adversity. Here's a closer look:

Cultivating Resilience: Resilience is the ability to bounce back from setbacks and challenges. Develop a mindset that views challenges as opportunities for growth and learning.

Embracing Adaptability: Recognize that change is a constant in the business world. Embrace adaptability as a skill that allows you to adjust to new circumstances, whether it's changes in client demands or shifts in industry trends.

Positive Mindset: Maintain a positive outlook even when facing difficult situations. Focus on solutions rather than dwelling on problems.

Learning from Failure: Approach failures as valuable learning experiences. Analyze what went wrong, identify lessons, and use that knowledge to make informed decisions moving forward.

Resilience Redefined: Alex's Journey of Adaptation in Consulting

Alex, a management consultant, faced a significant challenge when a key client unexpectedly terminated their contract. Instead of viewing it as a setback, Alex saw an opportunity to diversify his client portfolio and expand into new industries. He embraced adaptability by learning about the needs of different sectors and tailoring his services accordingly. Alex's resilience and adaptability not only helped him recover from the loss of a major client but also positioned him for long-term growth.

By developing resilience and adaptability, you're equipping yourself with the mental and emotional tools to navigate challenges and setbacks effectively. These qualities allow you to maintain your consultancy's forward momentum, even in the face of adversity, and position you to seize opportunities for growth and innovation.

Objective 3: Effective Problem Solving and Decision Making

This objective centers on honing your problem-solving skills and developing a structured approach to making well-informed decisions, especially when faced with challenges. Let's dive into the specifics:

Refine Problem-Solving Skills: Enhance your ability to analyze complex situations, identify root causes of challenges, and formulate effective solutions. This involves critical thinking and a methodical approach.

Structured Decision Making: Develop a structured process for making decisions under pressure. This might involve gathering relevant information, weighing pros and cons, and considering potential outcomes.

Consider Multiple Perspectives: When addressing challenges, consider various viewpoints and gather input from team members, clients, and stakeholders. This comprehensive approach leads to more well-rounded solutions.

Risk Assessment: Assess the potential risks and benefits of each solution before making a decision. Understanding potential consequences helps you make informed choices.

Data Dilemma to Informed Decision: Maria's Financial Consulting Triumph

Maria, a financial consultant, faced a challenging situation when a client requested a quick financial analysis with limited data. Instead of making hasty decisions, Maria gathered as much information as possible and considered various approaches. She consulted with her team members to gain diverse perspectives. By taking a structured approach, she was able to provide the client with a well-informed analysis that addressed their immediate needs while also outlining potential risks.

By mastering effective problem-solving and decision-making skills, you're better equipped to navigate challenges with confidence. Your ability to analyze situations, consider multiple perspectives, and make informed choices enhances your consultancy's agility and resilience. This objective empowers you to address challenges head-on and make decisions that contribute to your consultancy's sustainability and success.

Objective 4: Mitigate Risks and Uncertainties

This objective revolves around understanding the importance of risk management in maintaining your consultancy's sustainability and taking strategic steps to identify, assess, and mitigate potential risks and uncertainties. Here's a closer look:

Importance of Risk Management: Recognize that every consultancy operates in an environment of inherent uncertainties and potential risks. Effective risk management helps protect your consultancy's reputation, finances, and client relationships.

Identify Risks: Take a proactive approach by identifying potential risks that could impact your consultancy's operations, projects, and clients. These risks could include financial, operational, legal, or market-related uncertainties.

Assess and Prioritize: Evaluate the potential impact and likelihood of each identified risk. Prioritize risks based on their significance to your consultancy's goals and activities.

Develop Mitigation Strategies: Once risks are identified and assessed, develop strategies to mitigate or minimize their impact. This might involve contingency plans, preventative measures, or insurance coverage.

Continuous Monitoring: Recognize that risk management is an ongoing process. Regularly review and update your risk assessment and mitigation strategies to ensure they remain relevant.

Navigating Technical Waters: James' Journey to Effective Risk Management in Consulting

James, a technology consultant, understood the importance of risk management after a project he was involved in faced unexpected delays due to technical issues. He realized that he needed to identify potential technical risks early in the project lifecycle. James implemented a thorough risk assessment process that involved identifying potential technical challenges, assessing their impact, and developing contingency plans. As a result, he was better prepared to address unforeseen technical hurdles, ensuring that projects were delivered on time and within scope.

By mitigating risks and uncertainties, you're safeguarding your consultancy's stability and sustainability. A proactive approach to risk management enhances your ability to navigate challenges while preserving your consultancy's reputation and client trust. This objective equips you with tools to anticipate and address potential pitfalls, allowing you to steer your consultancy toward a future of controlled growth and success.

Objective 5: Maintain Ethical Integrity

This objective revolves around prioritizing ethical considerations in every aspect of your consultancy's operations. It's about building a reputation for ethical conduct that fosters trust, credibility, and long-term client relationships. Let's delve into the specifics:

Ethics in Decision Making: Make ethical considerations a core component of your decision-making process. Evaluate potential actions not only based on their legality but also on their ethical implications.

Transparency: Maintain open and transparent communication with clients, team members, and stakeholders. Being forthright about your actions and intentions builds trust.

Client Interactions: Treat clients with honesty, fairness, and respect. Avoid conflicts of interest, and ensure that clients' best interests are always at the forefront of your recommendations.

Confidentiality: Uphold client confidentiality by safeguarding sensitive information. Demonstrate your commitment to data privacy and security.

Compliance: Familiarize yourself with relevant laws, regulations, and industry standards that apply to your consultancy. Adhering to legal and ethical standards is crucial for maintaining your consultancy's reputation.

Ethical Compass: Jennifer's Uphold of Integrity in Legal Consulting

Jennifer, a legal consultant, faced a dilemma when a client requested advice that could potentially exploit a legal loophole. Instead of providing advice that might not align with ethical standards, Jennifer chose to explain the legal implications of the situation honestly, even if it meant losing the client. Her commitment to ethical integrity not only preserved her professional reputation but also earned her respect among clients who value honesty and transparency.

By maintaining ethical integrity, you're building a consultancy that clients can trust. Ethical conduct not only enhances your consultancy's credibility but also positions you as a responsible and respected industry professional. Upholding ethical principles in every facet of your consultancy's operations ensures that your long-term sustainability is built on a foundation of trust and ethical excellence.

Objective 6: Plan for Long-Term Sustainability

This objective is all about envisioning the future of your consultancy and developing a strategic plan that ensures its longevity. It involves considering various factors, from succession planning to growth strategies, and preparing for evolving market dynamics. Here's a closer look:

Strategic Vision: Develop a clear vision for where you want your consultancy to be in the long term. This vision guides your decision-making and helps you set achievable goals.

Succession Planning: Consider the future leadership of your consultancy. Whether you plan to pass the business to a successor or create a team to take over, succession planning ensures a smooth transition.

Growth Strategies: Explore strategies for sustainable growth, such as entering new markets, expanding service offerings, or targeting different client segments.

Market Analysis: Continuously assess market trends, client needs, and industry shifts. Adapt your strategies to align with changing market dynamics.

Financial Sustainability: Ensure your consultancy's financial stability by managing cash flow, budgeting effectively, and making prudent financial decisions.

Telehealth Trailblazer: Mark's Visionary Journey in Healthcare Consulting

Mark, a healthcare consultant, had a long-term vision of expanding his consultancy's services to include telemedicine solutions. He created a strategic plan that outlined the steps required to enter the telemedicine market, including regulatory compliance, technology integration, and client outreach. Mark also identified potential successors within his team and began mentoring them to eventually take on leadership roles. His proactive approach to long-term planning ensured the sustained growth and impact of his consultancy.

By planning for long-term sustainability, you're positioning your consultancy for continued success even as the business landscape evolves. Your strategic vision, succession planning, growth strategies, and financial stability lay the foundation for a consultancy that thrives for years to come, leaving a lasting legacy in your industry.

Navigating Challenges and Crafting a Lasting Legacy

As we conclude Chapter 7, you've embarked on a journey that uncovers the intricacies of consultancy—navigating challenges and securing the long-term sustainability of your practice. The objectives explored—identifying common challenges, developing resilience, effective problem solving, mitigating risks, maintaining ethical integrity, and planning for sustainability—have illuminated the path to a consultancy that not only survives but thrives.

Your ability to recognize challenges, adapt to change, and make informed decisions underscores your consultancy's agility and capacity to overcome obstacles. The cultivation of resilience equips you to weather storms and emerge stronger. Effective problem solving enhances your consultancy's problem-solving capabilities and its ability to provide innovative solutions.

Mitigating risks ensures the stability of your consultancy's operations, while maintaining ethical integrity fosters trust and credibility among clients and peers. And by planning for long-term sustainability, you're crafting a legacy that will continue to make an impact well into the future.

As you move forward, the culmination of these objectives positions you to lead your consultancy with unwavering confidence. You possess the skills, mindset, and strategies to navigate challenges, provide exceptional value to clients, and shape the future of your industry. The challenges you encounter today are the stepping stones to your consultancy's enduring success—a legacy that echoes your expertise, integrity, and commitment to making a meaningful difference.

Chapter 8: Cultivating Innovation and Staying Ahead

Welcome to Chapter 8, where we delve into the dynamic world of innovation and explore strategies for keeping your consultancy at the forefront of your industry. In this chapter, we will unravel the concept of innovation, its practical applications, and its role in driving your consultancy's growth. The objectives for this chapter are as follows:

Objectives:

Understanding Innovation and Its Significance:

- Gain a comprehensive understanding of what innovation entails in the context of consultancy.
- Recognize how innovation contributes to your consultancy's competitive edge and relevance.

Fostering a Culture of Innovation:

- Learn how to nurture an environment that encourages creative thinking and idea generation within your consultancy.
- Understand the importance of involving your team in the innovation process.

Identifying Opportunities for Innovation:

- Develop a keen eye for spotting areas where innovation can bring added value to your consultancy's services.
- Explore ways to leverage emerging technologies and trends to stay ahead.

Driving Innovation in Service Offerings:

- Explore methods to infuse innovation into your consultancy's service offerings to enhance client experiences.
- Learn how to tailor innovative solutions to meet unique client needs.

Embracing Technological Advancements:

- Keep up with the latest technological advancements that are relevant to your consultancy's domain.

- Understand how technology can streamline operations and elevate service quality.

Overcoming Innovation Barriers:

- Identify common obstacles that can hinder innovation within your consultancy.
- Develop strategies to overcome resistance to change and foster a more innovative mindset.

Through these objectives, you'll gain insights into the power of innovation and its potential to shape the trajectory of your consultancy. By embracing a culture of innovation, identifying opportunities for growth, and leveraging technology, you'll be poised to lead your consultancy into a future of continual evolution and success.

Objective 1: Understanding Innovation and Its Significance

This objective revolves around comprehending the concept of innovation within the context of consultancy and recognizing its role in maintaining your consultancy's competitive edge and relevance.

Let's delve into the specifics:

Defining Innovation: Understand that innovation goes beyond inventing new products or technologies. It involves creating novel approaches, processes, and solutions that provide unique value to clients.

Innovation's Impact: Recognize that innovation is a key driver of growth and differentiation in the consultancy industry. It allows you to stand out in a crowded market and meet evolving client expectations.

Types of Innovation: Explore different forms of innovation, such as process innovation (improving how tasks are performed), product innovation (introducing new offerings), and business model innovation (changing the way you deliver value).

Continuous Improvement: Realize that innovation isn't limited to radical changes; it can also involve incremental improvements that enhance your consultancy's services and client experiences.

Innovation Unleashed: Susan's Game-Changing Journey in Strategy Consulting

Susan, a strategy consultant, understood the significance of innovation in her consultancy. She introduced a new approach to client engagement by incorporating interactive workshops and immersive experiences. This innovative approach not only engaged clients more deeply but also led to more collaborative problem-solving. By embracing innovation, Susan transformed her consultancy's service delivery and positioned herself as a thought leader in her field.

By grasping the concept of innovation and its importance, you're laying the foundation for a consultancy that remains relevant and adaptable. Innovation empowers you to anticipate and meet changing client needs, ensuring that your consultancy remains at the forefront of industry trends and maintains a distinct competitive advantage.

Objective 2: Fostering a Culture of Innovation

This objective is centered on creating an environment within your consultancy that encourages creative thinking, idea generation, and the pursuit of innovative solutions. Here's a deeper dive into the specifics:

Encourage Open Communication: Foster a culture where team members feel comfortable sharing their ideas and insights. Create channels for open dialogue and encourage brainstorming sessions.

Value Diversity: Recognize the importance of diverse perspectives in sparking innovation. Embrace a diverse team that brings a range of experiences and viewpoints to the table.

Empowerment and Autonomy: Provide team members with the autonomy to explore new ideas and take ownership of innovative projects. Encourage them to experiment and take calculated risks.

Reward Creativity: Recognize and celebrate innovative efforts within your team. Consider implementing reward systems that acknowledge and incentivize creative thinking.

Leadership Buy-In: As a leader, set an example by actively participating in the innovation process. Demonstrate your commitment to innovation through your actions and decisions.

Designing Innovation: David's Path to a Creative Culture in Consultancy

David, a design consultant, believed in fostering a culture of innovation within his consultancy. He organized regular "innovation sessions" where team members from different departments came together to brainstorm and collaborate on new ideas. David also encouraged his team to explore unconventional approaches to design projects, which led to innovative solutions that impressed clients. By valuing creativity and providing a safe space for experimentation, David's consultancy became known for its innovative design concepts.

By cultivating a culture of innovation, you're creating an environment where creative thinking is nurtured and valued. This approach not only empowers your team to contribute to innovative solutions but also positions your consultancy as a hub of fresh ideas and forward-thinking strategies.

Objective 3: Identifying Opportunities for Innovation

This objective involves developing the ability to identify areas where innovation can enhance your consultancy's services and provide added value to your clients. Let's explore the specifics in more detail:

Client Needs Analysis: Analyze your clients' evolving needs and challenges. Look for gaps where innovative solutions can address pain points and provide unique benefits.

Industry Trends: Stay informed about emerging trends in your industry. Identify opportunities to leverage these trends to create innovative service offerings.

Market Research: Conduct thorough market research to understand the competitive landscape and identify areas where your consultancy can differentiate itself through innovation.

Feedback and Insights: Gather feedback from clients and team members. Their insights can highlight areas where innovative approaches can make a significant impact.

Cross-Disciplinary Insights: Seek inspiration from fields outside your own. Cross-disciplinary insights can lead to fresh perspectives and innovative ideas.

Sustainability Solutions: Rachel's Innovative Toolkit for Eco-Friendly Supply Chains

Rachel, a sustainability consultant, noticed that many of her clients were struggling with incorporating sustainable practices into their supply chains. Recognizing this need, she developed an innovative "Sustainability Integration Toolkit" that provided step-by-step guidance for incorporating eco-friendly practices into supply chain operations. This innovative offering not only addressed a common industry challenge but also positioned Rachel's consultancy as a leader in sustainable business solutions.

By identifying opportunities for innovation, you're aligning your consultancy with current and future client needs. Your ability to spot areas where innovative solutions can create value enhances your consultancy's relevance and distinguishes you as a consultant who is attuned to the evolving demands of your industry.

Objective 4: Driving Innovation in Service Offerings

This objective focuses on infusing innovation into your consultancy's service offerings to enhance client experiences and provide solutions that stand out in the market. Here's a closer look at the specifics:

Client-Centric Approach: Understand your clients' unique needs and preferences. Tailor innovative solutions that align with their goals and challenges.

Customization: Offer customizable service packages that allow clients to choose the components that best suit their requirements. This flexibility showcases your consultancy's willingness to adapt and innovate.

Value Enhancement: Identify areas where innovative enhancements can elevate the value you provide to clients. This could involve incorporating advanced technologies, streamlined processes, or unique methodologies.

Pilot Projects: Introduce pilot projects that showcase your innovative ideas in action. This gives clients a tangible experience of the value your innovations can bring.

Feedback Loop: Collect feedback from clients who have experienced your innovative service offerings. Use their insights to refine and improve your offerings over time.

Marketing Evolution: Kevin's Innovation Lab Redefining Consultancy

Kevin, a marketing consultant, recognized the need to innovate his service offerings to stand out in a competitive market. He introduced an "Innovation Lab" service, where clients could collaborate with his team to co-create cutting-edge marketing campaigns. This unique offering allowed clients to be part of the creative process and resulted in highly personalized and impactful campaigns. The Innovation Lab became a signature service that differentiated Kevin's consultancy from others in the industry.

By driving innovation in your service offerings, you're demonstrating your consultancy's commitment to staying ahead of the curve and providing exceptional value to clients. Innovative solutions not only solve problems but also create memorable experiences that clients remember and appreciate, fostering long-term relationships and positive word-of-mouth referrals.

Objective 5: Embracing Technological Advancements

This objective revolves around staying up-to-date with the latest technological advancements relevant to your consultancy's domain and leveraging technology to streamline operations and elevate service quality. Here's a closer look at the specifics:

Continuous Learning: Keep yourself informed about technological advancements in your industry. Attend workshops, conferences, and training sessions to stay up-to-date.

Relevance Assessment: Evaluate which technological advancements are most relevant to your consultancy's services and client needs. Focus on technologies that can bring tangible benefits

Integration Strategy: Develop a strategy for integrating technology into your consultancy's operations. Consider how new tools and systems can enhance efficiency, communication, and client interactions.

Enhanced Services: Explore how technology can enhance the services you provide. This could involve data analytics, automation, virtual collaboration tools, and more.

Efficiency Gains: Use technology to streamline processes and reduce manual work. This not only saves time but also allows you to allocate resources more effectively.

Tech-Driven HR Transformation: Emily's Journey to Modern Consultancy

Emily, an HR consultant, recognized the potential of technology to revolutionize her consultancy's operations. She adopted an AI-powered recruitment software that streamlined candidate screening and selection. This allowed her team to focus more on personalized interactions with clients and candidates, resulting in higher-quality matches. Emily's consultancy gained a reputation for using cutting-edge technology to deliver exceptional HR solutions.

By embracing technological advancements, you're harnessing the power of innovation to enhance your consultancy's offerings and operations. Technology can amplify your consultancy's impact, improve client experiences, and position you as a consultant who is at the forefront of industry trends.

Objective 6: Overcoming Innovation Barriers

This objective is focused on identifying and addressing common obstacles that can hinder the process of innovation within your consultancy. Let's dive into the specifics:

Resistance to Change: Recognize that individuals may be resistant to adopting new ideas or approaches. Understand the reasons behind this resistance and work to address concerns.

Cultural Barriers: Address cultural factors that might impede innovation, such as a hierarchical structure that discourages open communication or a fear of failure.

Lack of Resources: Overcome challenges related to limited budget, time, or expertise by seeking creative solutions, collaborating with external partners, or prioritizing key initiatives.

Risk Aversion: Understand that fear of failure can deter innovation. Create a culture where calculated risks are encouraged and failures are seen as learning opportunities.

Silos and Communication: Break down silos within your consultancy to encourage cross-functional collaboration. Effective communication and sharing of ideas can lead to innovative breakthroughs.

Breaking Barriers: Thomas' Path to Innovative Project Management in Consulting

Thomas, a management consultant, faced resistance from some team members when he proposed a new approach to project management. To overcome this resistance, he held open forums to discuss the benefits and address concerns. He also encouraged team members to share their ideas and engage in brainstorming sessions. By fostering an environment of open communication and collaboration, Thomas overcame barriers and successfully introduced an innovative project management process.

By proactively addressing innovation barriers, you're setting the stage for a more creative and forward-thinking consultancy. Overcoming resistance, fostering a culture of collaboration, and nurturing an environment that embraces calculated risks can unleash the full potential of your team's innovative thinking and drive your consultancy's growth and success.

Pioneering Innovation for Lasting Success

In closing Chapter 8, you've embarked on a transformative journey through the realm of innovation—an essential element in propelling your consultancy to new heights of success. The objectives explored—understanding innovation's significance, fostering an innovative culture, identifying opportunities, driving innovation in services, embracing technology, and overcoming barriers—have illuminated the path to becoming an innovative leader in your field.

Your grasp of innovation's role in consultancy, coupled with your commitment to nurturing a culture of creativity, lays the groundwork for a consultancy that thrives on fresh ideas and groundbreaking solutions. By identifying opportunities for innovation, you're positioning your consultancy as a trailblazer that continuously provides value to clients.

Driving innovation within your services showcases your consultancy's adaptability and readiness to meet ever-evolving client needs. Embracing technology not only streamlines operations but also ensures that your consultancy remains relevant and efficient.

As you overcome innovation barriers, you're proving your resilience and determination to forge ahead, regardless of challenges. Your consultancy's journey is one of innovation-driven growth—a journey that not only shapes your consultancy's future but also reshapes the industry landscape itself.

In the chapters ahead, we'll delve into further strategies to refine your consultancy's practices, overcome obstacles, and cement your position as an industry pioneer. The innovative spirit you've cultivated positions you on the cusp of transformative change—a change that propels your consultancy towards an inspiring and innovative future.

Chapter 9: Navigating Change and Evolving Strategies

Welcome to Chapter 9, where we dive into the dynamic landscape of change management and evolving strategies for your consultancy's sustained success. This chapter is a guide to effectively navigating change, adapting to new circumstances, and refining your strategies to remain ahead of the curve. The objectives for this chapter are as follows:

Objectives:

Understanding the Dynamics of Change:

- Gain insights into the nature of change and its impact on your consultancy.
- Recognize the importance of embracing change as a constant force in the business world.

Developing a Change-Ready Mindset:

- Cultivate a mindset that embraces change as an opportunity for growth and innovation.
- Overcome resistance to change and promote a culture of adaptability within your consultancy.

Managing Change Effectively:

- Learn strategies for managing change within your consultancy's operations and projects.
- Understand the role of communication and transparency in easing the transition.

Evolving Business Strategies:

- Explore the necessity of adapting your business strategies in response to changing market dynamics.
- Develop approaches for refining your consultancy's offerings and approaches to meet evolving client needs.

Agile Decision Making:

- Embrace agile decision-making processes that allow you to respond quickly to changing circumstances.
- Develop strategies for balancing thoughtful analysis with the need for timely action.

Leveraging Innovation for Adaptation:

- Understand how innovation can be leveraged to drive adaptation and change within your consultancy.
- Explore ways to infuse innovative thinking into your strategies for flexibility and growth.

Through these objectives, you'll gain the insights and tools needed to navigate the winds of change with confidence. By embracing change as an opportunity, refining your strategies, and leveraging innovation, you'll position your consultancy for continued success in an ever-evolving business landscape.

Objective 1: Understanding the Dynamics of Change

This objective revolves around gaining a comprehensive understanding of the nature of change and its impact on your consultancy. It's about recognizing that change is a constant force in the business world and appreciating the significance of embracing change as a necessary and transformative element. Here's a closer look:

Nature of Change: Understand that change is an inherent part of any industry. Market trends, client preferences, and external factors can shift rapidly, requiring adaptability.

Impact of Change: Recognize that change can disrupt established routines, processes, and strategies. It can create both challenges and opportunities for growth and improvement.

Embracing Change: Acknowledge that embracing change is not merely reactive but proactive. By embracing change as a catalyst for innovation, you position your consultancy for greater agility and resilience.

Continuous Learning: Commit to ongoing learning and staying informed about industry trends and emerging technologies. This knowledge equips you to anticipate and respond to changes effectively.

Adaptive Leadership: Olivia's Journey in Crafting Innovative Virtual Development

Olivia, a leadership development consultant, noticed a shift in client preferences toward more personalized and remote learning experiences. Rather than resisting this change, she embraced it by creating innovative virtual workshops and coaching sessions. Her consultancy's ability to adapt to this change not only retained existing clients but also attracted a new segment seeking flexible learning solutions.

By understanding the dynamics of change, you're better equipped to navigate shifts in the business landscape. Embracing change as an opportunity rather than a hindrance allows you to position your consultancy as a forward-thinking entity that is always prepared to evolve and meet the changing needs of your clients and the market.

Objective 2: Developing a Change-Ready Mindset

This objective is focused on cultivating a mindset within your consultancy that not only embraces change but also sees it as an opportunity for growth, innovation, and adaptation. Let's delve into the specifics:

Shift in Perspective: Transition from viewing change as a disruption to seeing it as a chance for exploration and improvement. A change-ready mindset sees challenges as stepping stones to progress.

Embrace Adaptability: Recognize that adaptability is a key trait in navigating change successfully. Encourage team members to be open to new ideas, approaches, and ways of working.

Communication and Engagement: Promote open communication about the importance of embracing change. Involve your team in decision-making processes, making them feel invested in the changes.

Learning from Failure: Foster an environment where failure is viewed as a valuable learning opportunity. Encourage experimentation and applaud efforts, even if they don't always yield the desired outcomes.

Remote Resilience: Michael's Transformational Journey in IT Consulting

Michael, an IT consultant, faced a major challenge when his consultancy needed to transition to remote work due to unforeseen circumstances. Rather than resisting the change, Michael encouraged his team to view it as an opportunity to explore new ways of collaborating and delivering services. He organized virtual brainstorming sessions and encouraged team members to share their insights and experiences. This change-ready mindset not only ensured a smooth transition but also led to the discovery of more efficient remote work practices.

By instilling a change-ready mindset within your consultancy, you're equipping your team with the ability to navigate change confidently. This mindset empowers your team to adapt to new circumstances, proactively seek solutions, and foster a culture of continuous improvement, ultimately contributing to your consultancy's resilience and long-term success.

Objective 3: Managing Change Effectively

This objective centers on acquiring the strategies and tools needed to manage change within your consultancy's operations and projects. Effective change management involves ensuring a smooth transition, minimizing disruption, and maintaining open communication. Here's a closer look:

Clear Communication: Communicate the reasons for change, its potential benefits, and the expected outcomes. Transparency fosters understanding and reduces uncertainty.

Engage Stakeholders: Involve key stakeholders, including team members and clients, in the change management process. Their input and buy-in are crucial for successful implementation.

Change Champions: Identify individuals within your consultancy who can champion the change. These change champions can help motivate and guide others through the transition.

Training and Support: Provide necessary training to equip your team with the skills needed for the change. Offer support and resources to address any challenges that may arise.

Feedback Mechanism: Create a feedback mechanism that allows team members and clients to share their thoughts, concerns, and suggestions throughout the change process.

Navigating Change: Sarah's Journey in Introducing Innovative Project Management

Sarah, a project management consultant, introduced a new project management software to enhance collaboration and efficiency. She conducted training sessions for her team, addressing their questions and concerns. Sarah also assigned a change champion in each team to assist with the transition and provide peer support. By actively managing the change, Sarah's consultancy smoothly integrated the new software while maintaining productivity.

By effectively managing change, you're ensuring that transitions within your consultancy are well-planned and executed. Open communication, stakeholder engagement, and support mechanisms lay the groundwork for a successful change process, allowing your consultancy to adapt to new circumstances while minimizing disruptions.

Objective 4: Evolving Business Strategies

This objective focuses on the necessity of adapting your business strategies in response to changing market dynamics, client needs, and industry trends. It's about staying nimble and continuously refining your consultancy's offerings and approaches to remain relevant and competitive. Let's explore the specifics:

Market Analysis: Regularly assess market trends, competitive landscape, and emerging opportunities. This analysis guides the evolution of your consultancy's strategies.

Client-Centric Approach: Align your strategies with the evolving needs and preferences of your clients. Tailor your services to address their challenges and goals.

Diversification: Explore opportunities to diversify your service offerings or target new client segments. This reduces your vulnerability to market shifts.

Innovation Integration: Integrate innovation into your strategies by incorporating creative solutions and novel approaches that set your consultancy apart.

Agility and Flexibility: Develop strategies that allow your consultancy to pivot quickly in response to changing circumstances, maintaining your competitive edge.

Supply Chain Sustainability Trailblazer: Alex's Evolution in Consulting

Alex, a sustainability consultant, noticed a growing demand for sustainable supply chain solutions among his clients. He evolved his business strategy by expanding his consultancy's services to include comprehensive supply chain audits and eco-friendly sourcing strategies. This strategic shift not only attracted new clients but also positioned Alex's consultancy as a leader in sustainable business practices

By evolving your business strategies, you're ensuring that your consultancy remains relevant and resilient in the face of change. Adapting to new market dynamics and client demands demonstrates your consultancy's ability to stay ahead and provide innovative solutions that meet the evolving needs of your clients.

Objective 5: Agile Decision Making

This objective is centered on adopting agile decision-making processes that enable you to respond quickly and effectively to changing circumstances. It's about striking a balance between thoughtful analysis and timely action to navigate uncertainties and make informed decisions. Let's explore the specifics:

Real-Time Data: Gather real-time data and insights to inform your decision-making. Use tools and analytics to gain a clear understanding of current trends and conditions.

Scenario Planning: Develop scenarios that outline different potential outcomes based on various factors. This helps you anticipate and prepare for different possibilities.

Cross-Functional Collaboration: Involve team members from different departments in decision-making processes. Diverse perspectives contribute to well-rounded decisions.

Test and Learn: Embrace a culture of experimentation. Test new strategies, approaches, or offerings on a small scale to gauge their effectiveness before full implementation.

Iterative Approach: Adopt an iterative approach to decision-making, where you make incremental adjustments based on feedback and evolving circumstances.

Strategic Agility: Emily's Methodical Approach to Consultancy Expansion

Emily, a business consultant, faced a decision regarding the expansion of her consultancy's services to a new market. Instead of making a rushed decision, she gathered market data, engaged in discussions with her team, and conducted a pilot project to test the waters. This agile decision-making process allowed her to assess the viability of the expansion and make informed adjustments based on real-world feedback.

By embracing agile decision-making, you're equipping your consultancy with the ability to respond swiftly to changes and make informed choices. This approach enhances your consultancy's adaptability and enables you to seize emerging opportunities while effectively managing risks and uncertainties.

Objective 6: Leveraging Innovation for Adaptation

This objective revolves around harnessing the power of innovation to drive adaptation and change within your consultancy. It's about infusing innovative thinking into your strategies to enhance flexibility, responsiveness, and growth. Let's delve into the specifics:

Innovative Mindset: Cultivate an innovative mindset within your team. Encourage them to think creatively, challenge assumptions, and explore new possibilities

Pilot Innovation: Introduce pilot projects that test innovative ideas in a controlled environment. Assess their impact and gather insights to refine your strategies.

Iterative Innovation: Embrace an iterative approach to innovation, where you continually refine and enhance your strategies based on feedback and outcomes.

Risk-Taking Culture: Foster a culture where calculated risks are encouraged and failures are seen as valuable learning experiences.

Feedback Loop: Establish mechanisms for collecting feedback from team members, clients, and stakeholders. Use this feedback to drive ongoing innovation.

AI Advancement: Marcus' Innovation Lab Driving Technology Consulting

Marcus, a technology consultant, recognized the need to adapt his consultancy's services to the rapid advancements in artificial intelligence. He introduced an "AI Innovation Lab" where his team collaborated on developing AI-driven solutions. This lab not only produced innovative products but also enhanced the consultancy's overall technical capabilities.

By leveraging innovation for adaptation, you're integrating creativity into the core of your consultancy's strategies. This approach ensures that your consultancy remains agile, open to change, and positioned to lead industry transformation. Innovation becomes the driving force that propels your consultancy's growth and sustains its relevance in a rapidly changing business landscape.

Chapter 10: Sustaining Growth and Leaving a Legacy

Welcome to Chapter 10, where we delve into the essential aspects of sustaining growth and creating a lasting legacy for your consultancy. This chapter is a guide to building upon your consultancy's success, nurturing its long-term viability, and establishing a reputation that stands the test of time. The objectives for this chapter are as follows:

Objectives:

Strategies for Sustained Growth:

- Explore strategies to ensure your consultancy's growth remains consistent and sustainable over time.
- Understand the importance of balancing short-term gains with long-term stability.

Cultivating Client Relationships:

- Learn how to foster strong and enduring relationships with clients.
- Recognize the role of trust, communication, and exceeding expectations in client retention.

Empowering Your Team:

- Develop approaches for nurturing a motivated and high-performing consultancy team.
- Understand the significance of investing in team development and fostering a collaborative environment.

Thought Leadership and Industry Impact:

- Explore how to position yourself and your consultancy as thought leaders in your industry.
- Understand the benefits of contributing to industry discussions and driving positive change.

Ethical Sustainability:

- Embrace ethical practices that sustain your consultancy's reputation and credibility.
- Explore how ethical decision-making impacts long-term success and client relationships.

Creating a Lasting Legacy:

- Develop a vision for the legacy you want your consultancy to leave behind.
- Understand how your actions today shape the impact your consultancy will have in the future.

Through these objectives, you'll uncover the strategies and principles that ensure your consultancy's growth, reputation, and impact continue to flourish. By embracing sustainability, nurturing relationships, and fostering innovation, you'll set the stage for your consultancy to become a true pillar of excellence in your industry.

Objective 1: Strategies for Sustained Growth

This objective focuses on exploring strategies that not only propel your consultancy's growth but also ensure that growth remains consistent and sustainable over the long term. It's about striking a balance between short-term gains and long-term stability. Let's delve into the specifics:

Diversification: Explore opportunities to diversify your service offerings or target new market segments. This reduces your dependency on a single source of revenue and enhances your consultancy's resilience.

Client Retention: Prioritize building lasting relationships with existing clients. Satisfied and loyal clients are more likely to engage your services repeatedly and refer new business.

Innovative Offerings: Continuously innovate your service offerings to meet evolving client needs. This positions your consultancy as a forward-thinking entity that anticipates market trends

Market Research: Conduct regular market research to identify emerging opportunities and potential threats. Staying informed allows you to adapt your strategies proactively.

Financial Prudence: Manage your consultancy's finances responsibly. Invest in growth while maintaining a financial cushion to weather unforeseen challenges.

Financial Expansion: Hannah's Journey into Diversified Consulting

Hannah, a financial consultant, recognized that her consultancy's growth was dependent on a narrow range of services. She diversified her offerings to include financial planning workshops for individuals and small businesses. This diversification not only expanded her client base but also provided a consistent revenue stream even during market fluctuations.

By implementing strategies for sustained growth, you're building a consultancy that thrives over the long haul.

Balancing short-term expansion with long-term stability ensures that your consultancy remains adaptable, resilient, and well-positioned to capitalize on emerging opportunities while navigating challenges.

Objective 2: Cultivating Client Relationships

This objective revolves around the art of fostering strong and enduring relationships with your clients. It's about going beyond transactional interactions and building connections based on trust, communication, and consistently exceeding expectations. Here's a closer look:

Client-Centric Approach: Prioritize your clients' needs and goals. Tailor your services to address their specific challenges and deliver value that resonates with them.

Open Communication: Foster transparent and open communication with your clients. Regularly update them on project progress, seek feedback, and address any concerns promptly.

Exceeding Expectations: Strive to consistently exceed your clients' expectations. Going the extra mile showcases your commitment to their success and fosters loyalty.

Anticipate Needs: Develop the ability to anticipate your clients' future needs. Proactively offer solutions and suggestions that demonstrate your expertise and dedication.

Building Trust: Trust is the cornerstone of enduring relationships. Deliver on your promises, be honest in your interactions, and demonstrate your consultancy's integrity.

Client-Centric Success: David's Recipe for Long-Lasting Consulting Relationships

David, a marketing consultant, maintained a strong relationship with a long-standing client by consistently delivering exceptional results and suggesting innovative strategies. He regularly scheduled check-ins to discuss progress and gather feedback, which allowed him to fine-tune his approach to align with the client's evolving goals.

By cultivating client relationships, you're not only ensuring repeat business but also fostering a network of advocates who refer new clients based on their positive experiences. These strong connections position your consultancy as a trusted partner in your clients' success stories.

Objective 3: Empowering Your Team

This objective focuses on developing approaches that empower and nurture a motivated and high-performing consultancy team. It's about recognizing that a cohesive and skilled team is essential for sustained growth and success. Let's delve into the specifics:

Professional Development: Invest in your team's growth by providing training, skill enhancement opportunities, and access to industry resources.

Collaborative Environment: Foster a collaborative atmosphere where team members are encouraged to share ideas, collaborate on projects, and learn from one another.

Clear Expectations: Set clear expectations for roles, responsibilities, and performance standards. This clarity promotes accountability and ensures everyone is aligned toward common goals.

Recognition and Rewards: Recognize and celebrate achievements within your team. Implement reward systems that acknowledge exceptional performance and contributions.

Effective Communication: Promote open and effective communication channels within your team. This enhances transparency, reduces misunderstandings, and encourages collaboration.

Empowering Excellence: Sarah's Leadership in Cultivating Team Synergy

Sarah, a leadership consultant, created a culture of empowerment within her consultancy by organizing regular team-building workshops, encouraging cross-functional collaboration, and providing her team with opportunities to attend leadership conferences. This approach not only boosted team morale but also resulted in a more cohesive and high-performing consultancy.

By empowering your team, you're nurturing a work environment that fosters innovation, dedication, and loyalty. A motivated and skilled team becomes an invaluable asset that propels your consultancy's growth, excellence, and ability to tackle challenges effectively.

Objective 4: Thought Leadership and Industry Impact

This objective revolves around positioning yourself and your consultancy as thought leaders within your industry. It's about sharing valuable insights, contributing to industry discussions, and driving positive change through your expertise. Let's delve into the specifics:

In-Depth Knowledge: Continuously deepen your expertise in your consultancy's domain. Stay informed about industry trends, emerging technologies, and best practices.

Content Creation: Share your knowledge through various mediums, such as blog posts, articles, webinars, and podcasts. Provide valuable insights that showcase your consultancy's thought leadership.

Public Speaking: Participate in industry events, conferences, and webinars as a speaker. Sharing your expertise in these forums establishes you as an authority in your field.

Networking: Build relationships with other thought leaders, professionals, and influencers in your industry. Collaborate on projects and engage in meaningful discussions.

Driving Change: Use your thought leadership to drive positive change within your industry. Advocate for ethical practices, innovative approaches, and industry improvements.

AI Authority: John's Thought Leadership in Technology Consulting

John, a technology consultant, actively shared his insights on the implications of artificial intelligence on businesses through blog posts and conference presentations. His thought leadership not only positioned him as an expert in AI but also led to collaborations with tech companies seeking his expertise.

By becoming a thought leader, you're elevating your consultancy's reputation and influence. Thought leadership enhances your visibility, attracts client

Objective 5: Ethical Sustainability

This objective centers on embracing ethical practices that sustain your consultancy's reputation and credibility over the long term. It's about making decisions that align with your values and positively impact your clients, team, and the broader community. Let's delve into the specifics:

Transparency: Operate with transparency in all your dealings. Communicate openly with clients, team members, and stakeholders, building trust and credibility.

Integrity: Uphold the highest standards of integrity in your consultancy's actions. Honesty and ethical behavior should guide every decision.

Client Welfare: Prioritize the well-being of your clients by providing services that genuinely benefit them and avoiding conflicts of interest.

Team Respect: Treat your team members with respect and fairness. Foster an inclusive environment that promotes diversity, equity, and work-life balance.

Community Engagement: Contribute positively to the community by supporting social and environmental initiatives. Engage in activities that align with your consultancy's values.

Ethical Sustainability: Mia's Stand for Environmental Responsibility in Consulting

Mia, a sustainability consultant, turned down a project that conflicted with her consultancy's values of environmental responsibility. This decision reinforced her commitment to ethical sustainability and positioned her consultancy as an advocate for environmentally friendly practices.

By embracing ethical sustainability, you're safeguarding your consultancy's reputation and credibility. Ethical practices build lasting relationships, inspire trust among clients and stakeholders, and demonstrate your consultancy's commitment to contributing positively to society.

Objective 6: Creating a Lasting Legacy

This objective is centered on developing a vision for the legacy you want your consultancy to leave behind. It's about understanding that your actions today shape the impact your consultancy will have in the future, and that your decisions can leave a meaningful and lasting imprint. Let's explore the specifics:

Long-Term Vision: Define the legacy you aspire to create for your consultancy. Consider the positive influence you want your consultancy to have on clients, team members, the industry, and beyond.

Values Alignment: Ensure that your consultancy's actions and decisions align with the legacy you envision. Every choice should reflect your consultancy's core values and long-term objectives.

Knowledge Sharing: Commit to sharing your expertise and insights to empower future generations of consultants and professionals.

Mentorship: Provide mentorship to emerging consultants, guiding them with your experience and wisdom.

Continuous Improvement: Strive for continuous improvement and adaptability, ensuring your consultancy remains relevant and impactful over time

Consulting Catalyst: Mark's Legacy of Empowering Future Leaders.

Mark, a management consultant, established a scholarship program that supported young individuals pursuing careers in consulting. His consultancy's legacy went beyond financial success—it became synonymous with nurturing talent and giving back to the industry.

By actively working towards creating a lasting legacy, you're elevating your consultancy's impact to a level that extends far beyond the present moment. Your actions become a testament to your values, expertise, and commitment to leaving the world a better place through your consultancy's endeavors.

Building a Legacy of Excellence

As we conclude Chapter 10, you've embarked on a journey to sustain growth, nurture relationships, empower your team, establish thought leadership, uphold ethical standards, and create a lasting legacy for your consultancy. The objectives explored—strategies for growth, client relationship cultivation, team empowerment, thought leadership, ethical sustainability, and legacy creation—have illuminated the path to cementing your consultancy's reputation as a beacon of excellence

By implementing sustainable growth strategies, you're laying the foundation for a consultancy that thrives while maintaining stability. Cultivating enduring client relationships and empowering your team ensures that your consultancy remains a trusted partner for clients and a nurturing environment for professionals.

Positioning yourself as a thought leader demonstrates your consultancy's expertise and willingness to contribute positively to your industry's discourse. Ethical sustainability, as a guiding principle, secures your consultancy's integrity and strengthens its connection to clients and stakeholders.

As you work towards leaving a lasting legacy, your consultancy's impact is magnified, and its influence extends far beyond immediate business transactions. The journey you're on is one of purpose, impact, and meaningful contribution—a legacy that shapes the industry, uplifts individuals, and leaves an indelible mark on the world.

With the principles and strategies outlined in this chapter, you're not just building a consultancy; you're building a legacy of excellence that inspires, empowers, and leaves a positive and enduring impact for generations to come.

Chapter 11: The Power of Adaptation and Resilience

Welcome to Chapter 11, where we delve into the essential concepts of adaptation and resilience as cornerstones of your consultancy's success. This chapter is a guide to harnessing the power of adaptability and building resilience to navigate challenges, seize opportunities, and thrive in a dynamic business landscape. The objectives for this chapter are as follows:

Objectives:

Understanding Adaptation: Explore the significance of adaptation in the face of changing circumstances and its role in maintaining relevance.

Building Resilience: Develop strategies to build resilience within your consultancy, ensuring its ability to withstand setbacks and emerge stronger.

Embracing Change: Cultivate a mindset that embraces change as a catalyst for growth and innovation.

Adapting to Market Trends: Learn how to monitor and respond to market trends effectively to remain competitive and agile.

Overcoming Challenges: Discover techniques for overcoming challenges and turning them into opportunities for improvement.

Fostering Innovation: Understand how adaptation and resilience fuel innovation within your consultancy's practices and approaches.

Through these objectives, you'll gain insights and tools to steer your consultancy through the ebb and flow of the business landscape

Objective 1: Understanding Adaptation

This objective centers on exploring the significance of adaptation in the context of your consultancy's success. It's about recognizing that in a world of constant change, the ability to adapt is not just a skill but a critical necessity. Let's delve into the specifics:

Change as Inevitable: Understand that change is a constant in any business environment. Market trends, client needs, and industry dynamics evolve over time.

Maintaining Relevance: Adaptation ensures your consultancy remains relevant in the face of shifting circumstances. Stagnation can lead to obsolescence, while adaptation keeps you in sync with the changing demands of the market.

Flexibility as Strength: View adaptability as a strength rather than a vulnerability. The ability to pivot and adjust to new situations enhances your consultancy's resilience.

Innovation Catalyst: Adaptation often sparks innovation. Embracing change can lead to the discovery of new ideas, approaches, and solutions.

Consulting Catalyst: Mark's Legacy of Empowering Future Leaders

Rachel, a digital marketing consultant, witnessed a shift in social media trends that favored visual content over text-based posts. Recognizing the need to adapt, she pivoted her consultancy's content strategy to include more visual elements. This adaptation not only retained her consultancy's online visibility but also attracted a broader audience.

By understanding the importance of adaptation, you're equipping your consultancy with the tools needed to respond effectively to change. Embracing adaptation as a continuous process ensures that your consultancy remains agile, relevant, and prepared to capitalize on new opportunities that arise.

Objective 2: Building Resilience

This objective revolves around developing strategies that build resilience within your consultancy, allowing it to withstand setbacks and emerge stronger from challenges. Resilience ensures that your consultancy can navigate uncertainties and maintain its course towards success. Here's a closer look:

Anticipating Challenges: Recognize potential challenges and proactively prepare for them. A resilient consultancy foresees obstacles and has contingency plans in place.

Adapting to Change: Resilience involves adapting to change without losing focus on your goals. Your consultancy can pivot while staying aligned with its core mission.

Learning from Setbacks: Embrace setbacks as opportunities for growth. Resilience enables you to learn from failures and turn them into valuable lessons.

Resource Management: Efficiently manage your consultancy's resources, including finances, human capital, and time. This preparedness contributes to resilience during tough times.

Resilient Revival: Jonathan's Journey in Adaptable Consulting

Jonathan, a management consultant, experienced a significant client project cancellation due to unforeseen budget cuts. His consultancy's resilience shone as he quickly reallocated resources, restructured his team, and pursued alternative revenue streams. This adaptability not only minimized the impact but also positioned his consultancy to emerge stronger.

By building resilience, you're equipping your consultancy to weather challenges with grace and strength. Resilience ensures that setbacks are temporary and that your consultancy can navigate obstacles while maintaining its forward momentum.

Objective 3: Embracing Change

This objective centers on cultivating a mindset that not only accepts change but also embraces it as a catalyst for growth and innovation. It's about shifting your perspective to view change as an opportunity rather than a disruption. Let's delve into the specifics:

Positive Mindset: Develop a positive attitude towards change. Rather than resisting it, approach change with curiosity and an open mind.

Adaptability: Cultivate the ability to adapt quickly to new circumstances. Embracing change allows your consultancy to stay relevant and agile.

Innovation Driver: Understand that change often sparks innovation. Embracing change encourages your team to think creatively and explore new approaches.

Continuous Learning: See change as an opportunity to learn and expand your consultancy's knowledge. Every change brings new insights and lessons.

Navigating Change: Lisa's Strategic Adaptation in Business Consulting

Lisa, a business strategy consultant, faced a significant change when her main client shifted its strategic direction. Instead of seeing this as a setback, Lisa embraced the change by researching the new industry trends and adapting her consultancy's services. This adaptation not only retained her client but also positioned her consultancy as a trusted partner for navigating industry shifts.

By embracing change as a catalyst for growth, you're setting the stage for your consultancy to thrive in dynamic environments. A mindset that welcomes change paves the way for continuous improvement, innovation, and an unwavering ability to seize emerging opportunities.

Objective 4: Adapting to Market Trends

This objective revolves around the ability to monitor and respond effectively to market trends, ensuring that your consultancy remains competitive and agile in a rapidly evolving business landscape. Adapting to market trends positions your consultancy to meet client needs and seize emerging opportunities. Let's explore the specifics:

Market Research: Regularly conduct thorough market research to identify emerging trends, client preferences, and industry shifts.

Anticipate Client Needs: Use market insights to anticipate your clients' evolving needs. Proactively adapt your services to align with these changing requirements.

Innovation Alignment: Align your consultancy's innovations with market trends. Your offerings should reflect the current demands of the industry.

Strategic Pivots: Be prepared to pivot your consultancy's strategies based on shifting market dynamics. Flexibility ensures you remain aligned with the changing business landscape.

Cybersecurity Trailblazer: Michael's Evolution in Technology Consulting

Michael, a technology consultant, noticed a growing demand for cybersecurity solutions due to an increase in cyber threats. He swiftly adapted his consultancy's service offerings to include comprehensive cybersecurity audits and training. This alignment with market trends not only attracted new clients but also established Michael's consultancy as an industry leader in cybersecurity.

By effectively adapting to market trends, you're positioning your consultancy as a responsive and forward-thinking entity. The ability to anticipate shifts and tailor your services to meet market demands ensures that your consultancy remains relevant, competitive, and well-equipped to address your clients' evolving challenges.

Objective 5: Overcoming Challenges

This objective is centered on discovering techniques for overcoming challenges and transforming them into opportunities for improvement and growth. It's about adopting a proactive approach to challenges and leveraging them to strengthen your consultancy's capabilities. Here's a closer look:

Resilience Mindset: Approach challenges with a resilient mindset. View them as opportunities to learn, adapt, and emerge stronger

Problem-Solving: Develop effective problem-solving skills within your team. Encourage creative thinking and collaborative approaches to tackle challenges.

Continuous Improvement: Use challenges as catalysts for continuous improvement. Identify areas that need enhancement and implement changes that lead to better outcomes.

Risk Management: Identify potential challenges early and develop strategies to mitigate risks. Being prepared minimizes the impact of unforeseen obstacles.

Resilient Reorganization: Sophia's Adaptive Leadership in Financial Consulting

Sophia, a financial consultant, faced a challenge when a key team member unexpectedly left during a critical project. Instead of panicking, she leveraged the situation as an opportunity for cross-training within her team. This not only ensured the project's completion but also created a more versatile and adaptable consultancy team.

By overcoming challenges, you're building a consultancy that thrives even in adversity. Challenges become stepping stones to growth, innovation, and increased resilience. Your consultancy's ability to turn obstacles into opportunities demonstrates your commitment to excellence and adaptability.

Objective 6: Fostering Innovation

This objective revolves around understanding how adaptation and resilience fuel innovation within your consultancy's practices and approaches. It's about recognizing that the process of adapting to change often leads to the discovery of new and innovative solutions. Let's delve into the specifics:

Creative Exploration: Encourage your team to think creatively when facing challenges. The need to adapt often sparks innovative thinking.

Flexibility and Experimentation: Embrace flexibility in your approaches. Be open to experimenting with new ideas, strategies, and solutions.

Learning from Adaptation: Recognize that the process of adaptation involves learning and improvement. These insights contribute to your consultancy's innovative capacity

Innovative Problem-Solving: Use adaptation as an opportunity to solve problems in novel ways. Your consultancy becomes a breeding ground for creative problem-solving.

Virtual Healthcare Visionary: Alex's Journey into Innovative Telehealth Consulting

Alex, a healthcare consultant, adapted his consultancy's operations to virtual platforms during a time when in-person interactions were limited. This adaptation led to the development of innovative telehealth solutions that expanded his consultancy's reach and services.

By fostering innovation through adaptation, you're creating a consultancy that thrives on ingenuity and forward-thinking. Adapting to change becomes not only a necessity but also a pathway to uncovering new opportunities, enhancing your offerings, and continually pushing the boundaries of what your consultancy can achieve.

Adapting and Thriving in a Dynamic World

As we conclude Chapter 11, you've explored the essential concepts of adaptation and resilience—the twin pillars that empower your consultancy to not only navigate challenges but also seize opportunities and flourish in a dynamic business landscape. The objectives covered— understanding adaptation, building resilience, embracing change, adapting to market trends, overcoming challenges, and fostering innovation—have illuminated the path to creating a consultancy that thrives amidst change.

By understanding that change is a constant and embracing it as an avenue for growth, you're equipping your consultancy with the tools needed to respond effectively to evolving circumstances. Building resilience ensures that setbacks become stepping stones, enabling your consultancy to emerge stronger from challenges.

A mindset that welcomes change fosters adaptability and innovation. By staying aligned with market trends, you position your consultancy as a responsive and forward-thinking entity, ready to cater to emerging needs. Overcoming challenges with creativity and resilience transforms obstacles into opportunities. Each challenge conquered becomes a chance for improvement and growth. As you nurture a culture of innovation through adaptation, your consultancy becomes a dynamic force that thrives on change, consistently evolving to meet the needs of a rapidly transforming world.

The journey you've undertaken in this chapter is one of empowerment, learning, and growth—a journey that equips your consultancy not only to survive but to thrive and lead in an ever-changing business landscape. Through adaptation and resilience, your consultancy emerges as a beacon of strength, agility, and excellence, ready to embrace whatever the future holds.

Chapter 12: Achieving Sustainable Success

Welcome to Chapter 12, where we explore the crucial aspects of achieving sustainable success for your consultancy. This chapter delves into strategies that go beyond short-term gains, focusing on creating a lasting impact that ensures your consultancy's longevity and prosperity. The objectives for this chapter are as follows:

Objectives:

Defining Sustainable Success: Understand what sustainable success means in the context of your consultancy and set clear benchmarks for achievement.

Holistic Growth: Explore approaches for holistic growth that encompass financial, social, and environmental aspects.

Long-Term Value Creation: Develop strategies to create long-term value for both clients and stakeholders, fostering enduring relationships.

Ethical Leadership: Embrace ethical leadership principles that guide your consultancy's decisions and actions.

Social Responsibility: Explore ways to contribute positively to society and communities through your consultancy's endeavors.

Legacy of Impact: Define the legacy of impact you want your consultancy to leave behind and align your actions accordingly.

Through these objectives, you'll gain insights into fostering sustainable success that transcends immediate achievements, ensuring your consultancy's positive influence endures over time.

Objective 1: Defining Sustainable Success

This objective centers on gaining a clear understanding of what sustainable success means for your consultancy and setting well-defined benchmarks to measure achievement. It's about moving beyond short-term profitability and embracing a holistic view of success that considers long-term viability and positive impact. Let's explore the specifics:

Clarifying Values: Define the core values and principles that underpin your consultancy's vision of success. These values will guide your decisions and actions.

Longevity and Impact: Consider how your consultancy's success can be sustained over the long term while making a positive impact on clients, stakeholders, and the industry.

Measurable Benchmarks: Establish measurable benchmarks that reflect different dimensions of success, such as financial growth, client satisfaction, and social responsibility.

Balancing Objectives: Strive to strike a balance between financial gains, ethical practices, and societal contributions. Sustainable success encompasses all these aspects.

Sustainability Success: Mary's Holistic Approach to Consulting Achievement

Mary, a sustainability consultant, defined sustainable success for her consultancy as achieving consistent financial growth while advancing eco-friendly practices and actively participating in community initiatives. She set measurable targets for each aspect and used them to assess her consultancy's progress.

By defining sustainable success, you're aligning your consultancy's goals with a vision that goes beyond immediate gains. This holistic approach ensures that your consultancy not only thrives financially but also leaves a lasting positive imprint on clients, stakeholders, and the world at large.

Objective 2: Holistic Growth

This objective revolves around exploring approaches that promote holistic growth for your consultancy. It's about recognizing that sustainable success encompasses financial prosperity, social responsibility, and environmental stewardship. Let's delve into the specifics:

Financial Health: Strive for financial growth and stability, ensuring your consultancy's ability to invest in innovation and weather challenges.

Social Impact: Consider how your consultancy's operations can positively impact society. Engage in initiatives that promote inclusivity, diversity, and community well-being.

Environmental Consciousness: Implement eco-friendly practices and reduce your consultancy's environmental footprint. Embrace sustainability in your operations and offerings.

Stakeholder Engagement: Foster strong relationships with clients, employees, investors, and the wider community. Holistic growth involves a collaborative approach that benefits all stakeholders.

Holistic Growth: Robert's Journey in Balancing People, Planet, and Profit

Robert, a management consultant, pursued holistic growth by incorporating remote work options for his team, reducing commuting-related emissions. Additionally, his consultancy partnered with local charities to support education initiatives, thereby contributing to the community's well-being.

By embracing holistic growth, your consultancy's success becomes a force for positive change across financial, social, and environmental dimensions. Balancing these aspects ensures that your consultancy's prosperity aligns with ethical practices and contributes to a better world.

Objective 4: Ethical Leadership

This objective centers on embracing ethical leadership principles that guide your consultancy's decisions and actions. It's about setting a standard of integrity, transparency, and responsible conduct that influences your consultancy's culture and interactions. Here's a closer look:

Integrity and Honesty: Uphold the highest standards of integrity in all your consultancy's dealings. Honest and ethical behavior sets the tone for your team and clients.

Transparency: Foster transparent communication within your consultancy. Openly sharing information builds trust and accountability.

Accountability: Hold yourself and your team accountable for ethical decisions and actions. Ethical leadership involves taking responsibility for both successes and mistakes.

Respect for Stakeholders: Treat clients, team members, investors, and other stakeholders with respect and fairness. Ethical leadership extends to how you interact with and treat others.

Ethical Leadership: Emily's Beacon of Trust in
Consulting

Emily, a leadership consultant, demonstrated ethical leadership by consistently communicating project timelines and progress with her clients. Her consultancy's commitment to transparent and honest communication earned her clients' trust and long-term partnerships.

By embracing ethical leadership, you're cultivating a consultancy that is not only successful but also respected and trusted by clients, employees, and stakeholders. Ethical principles become the foundation upon which your consultancy's reputation is built, positioning you as a leader who values integrity and responsible conduct.

In the final chapter of this book, we have explored the remarkable journeys of consultants who embraced change, innovation, adaptability, and ethical values to achieve exceptional success in their respective fields. These consultants didn't merely excel in their roles; they redefined the essence of consultancy itself.

Their stories serve as beacons of inspiration, highlighting the importance of not only delivering outstanding service but also embracing continuous improvement, ethical conduct, and a commitment to sustainability. These consultants not only achieved financial success but also made a lasting impact on their clients, industries, and communities.

As we conclude this book, remember that their journeys are not isolated instances. They represent a path that all consultants can embark upon—a path of growth, innovation, resilience, and ethical leadership. Whether you are a seasoned consultant or just starting on this journey, the lessons from these stories are a testament to the limitless potential within the world of consultancy.

As you close this book, consider how you can apply these lessons to your own consultancy journey. The road ahead may be challenging, but it is also filled with opportunities for growth, transformation, and the creation of a consultancy legacy that extends far beyond the balance sheet.

Thank you for joining us on this inspiring journey through the world of consultancy. May your own consultancy endeavors be marked by success, purpose, and positive impact.

www.ingramcontent.com/pod-product-compliance
Lightning Source LLC
Chambersburg PA
CBHW072202290526
45794CB00004B/1621